GW01071899

ONLY
BELIEVE

A MEMOIR

BY

RAY
BARNETT

ONLY BELIEVE

Copyright © 2017 by Ray Barnett

ISBN: 978-0-692-99338-5

All RIGHTS RESERVED

By Ray Barnett with Ingrid Ricks

Cover Design by Thea Chard

Book Formatting by Thea Chard

Image Credits:

TO MY MOTHER, LAVINA ROSS

Who took me into her heart and home, and raised me as one of her own. Her love, generosity and unwavering belief in me got me through the tough times as a child, and helped shape me into the person I am.

FOREWARD

MY LIFE AND MINISTRY has never taken an orderly path. Instead, it's been an ongoing quest with starts and stops and repeated steps into the unknown – always driven by my faith and continual guidance by God.

This book captures my story as best as I can tell it – from my childhood, to my ministry, to my ongoing quest to fully discover my family and identity.

While a big part of my ministry has been focused on the African Children's Choir, I only share a small piece of that story in this book because it's a story that requires a book of its own.

I'm currently working on that book and hope to have it completed within the next year.

MINISTRY TIMELINE

1966—Discovery of Persecuted and imprisoned Christians Behind Iron Curtain

1972—Launch of Friends in the West

1975—Launch Prayer Bracelets for Pastor Georgi Vins and other Imprisoned Christians

FALL 1975—Travel to Mozambique to Visit Salu Daka and other imprisoned missionaries

FALL 1976—Congressional Resolution Passes Condemning Soviet Union and Demanding Release of Pastor Georgi Vins

JANUARY 1977—Salu Daka released

SEPTEMBER 1978—Travel to Uganda to Meet with Persecuted Christians

SEPTEMBER 1978—Travel to East Berlin to meet with Wolfgang Vogel on behalf of Georgi Vins

APRIL 1979—Georgi Vins released

JUNE 1982—Launch of Lebanon Aid mission

SEPTEMBER 1984—Launch of African Children's Choir

SPRING 1986—Launch of Prayer Campaign for Lebanon hostages

SUMMER 1986—Began talks with Lebanese regarding hostages

NOVEMBER 1986—Release of hostage David Jacobsen

JANUARY 1987—Talks begin with Hezbollah leaders

DECEMBER 1991—Release of Terry Anderson and other remaining hostages

JUNE 1993—Kick off relief efforts and development projects in Southern Sudan; locate Lost Boys

FALL 1993—Initiate healing efforts in Rwanda on heels of genocide there

DECEMBER 2003—Initiate humanitarian aid, music therapy camps for AIDS orphans in Southern Africa

PROLOGUE

January 1987

ANXIETY SURGED THROUGH ME as my eyes locked on Sheik Mohammad Hussein Fadlallah, the most powerful Muslim cleric in Lebanon and rumored leader of Hezbollah—the Islamic organization allegedly responsible for kidnapping and imprisoning Westerners.

The plight of the Lebanon hostages was escalating and I had been asking God for guidance on how to help for months. I had launched a prayer campaign through my small Christian-based humanitarian organization, Friends in the West, and had produced and distributed thousands of prayer bracelets engraved with the names of the captives. I had also been involved in ongoing talks with Muslim friends living in Beirut. Now—thanks to relationships I had developed a few years earlier while operating a Lebanon Aid mission during Israel's invasion of the country—I had secured a meeting with the man I believed had the influence and connections to end the hostage crisis.

Sheik Fadlallah was watching me, waiting for me to speak. I had thought about this conversation the entire night, wondering what I could possibly say to start a dialogue that would eventually lead to the hostages' release. Ultimately I decided there was only one thing I could do: Tell the truth.

"I'm an evangelical Christian minister from Canada and I've started a prayer campaign for the hostages," I started out, silently praying that my words would connect with the Sheik. "I am a committed Christian and you are a committed Muslim. I'm wondering if there is anything we can talk about even though we are separated by our faith."

Though I concentrated on keeping my voice calm and steady, the tension was so unnerving I was struggling to breathe. I had felt it creeping into the air the day before as my flight neared the Beirut airport. A number of Westerners had vanished over the past few weeks and the flight attendant who had been servicing me was concerned.

"Mr. Barnett, we are from East Beirut. Would you like to ride in our bus from the airport?" she had asked, her face creased with worry. "It's very dangerous for you to go on your own through West Beirut."

I knew my trip was risky and that there was a chance I could disappear. But I had convinced myself that my friendships in the Muslim community offered at least some level of protection. Beyond that, I knew it was God's guidance that had brought me this far and though I could feel the adrenaline surging through me, I had faith that He would see me through.

"I'll be fine," I had assured the flight attendant, motioning to the Lebanese businessman seated across the aisle who had arranged the trip for me. "I'm with a friend and he's going to be looking out for me."

We exited the plane and were met on the tarmac by three men who asked for our passports and then ushered us into a posh black limousine to wait while they facilitated our clearance through customs.

A few minutes later they were back and drove us directly to the businessman's apartment. Two men armed with AK-47s greeted us and guarded the apartment overnight. These same men had driven us to

Sheik Fadlallah's heavily guarded compound and were now outside, waiting for us.

The Sheik remained silent while my colleague interpreted my words, though I had seen the recognition on his face as I talked and was convinced he had understood everything I said.

I concentrated on breathing as I waited for Sheik Fadlallah's response.

"Prayer is worship, worship is prayer, and everything we do day and night should be an act of worship," he said finally, pausing for my colleague to translate his words for me. "You being here this morning is an act of worship."

I could feel my body relaxing as I took in the Sheik's words. I knew it was a signal that he accepted me being there and that the door was open for ongoing communication.

That first meeting was primarily an introduction and a way to feel each other out. It was at our second meeting a few days later that Sheik Fadlallah sent a signal of his own to communicate what I already suspected.

"In my faith it's permitted for me to lie to you," he said coyly.

I let his words sink in and focused on keeping my tone measured when I replied.

"What would you be permitted to lie about?" I asked.

The Sheik smiled slightly.

"For example, if we were holding some people and others might try to kill them, we would protect them," he replied.

I was back at the apartment, trying to process and decipher the Sheik's words, when one of my guards motioned me over to the balcony.

"Look down there, Mr. Ray," he said. "That's Terry Waite eating an ice cream cone."

Terry Waite was an official for the Church of England who, according to media reports, was in Lebanon acting as a mediator on behalf of the hostages. It had been rumored that he was working in conjunction with the US government, though it was hard to know what was true.

"Oh," I said, looking down at Waite. "I read somewhere that he's negotiating for the hostages."

The guard smiled.

"He's not negotiating," he replied.

Two days later I was seated in the first-class cabin on a plane headed for London. I hadn't been scheduled to leave Beirut for another day and my ticket was supposed to route me through Kano, Nigeria, which is where I'd originated my trip. But that morning the armed men who had served as both my guards and hosts told me it was time to go.

"You need to leave today, Mr. Ray," one of the men said, pushing the first-class ticket to London into my hand. "We will take you now."

This time I wasn't ushered into a limousine. It was an ordinary car and as I climbed into the front passenger seat, I glanced behind me and noticed that the floor was covered in hand grenades. Neither the driver nor the armed guard seated in the back seat spoke as we drove, and though they had treated me like a revered guest during my stay in Beirut, I couldn't shake the thought that it was all a guise and I was being taken hostage after all.

I whispered a pleading prayer in my mind and concentrated on positive thoughts as the car sped down the highway.

I felt myself starting to relax when I saw signs for the airport. But as soon as we arrived at the entrance, a soldier in the Syrian army motioned for our car to stop. Within seconds, he was engaged in a heated argument with the armed man seated in the back seat.

Suddenly the man scooped up the grenades from the floor, shoved them in his pockets, and jumped out of the car.

Sirens screamed in my head.

"What's going on?" I asked my driver, hoping my voice didn't sound as alarmed as I felt.

"Oh, do not worry, Mr. Ray," he said. "Everything's fine. The army is just trying to clean up the airport, so they told us he would have to wait here with the gun and grenades.

"But do not worry," my driver repeated. "We told the soldier that if anything happens to you, he will pull the pin on the grenade and blow everyone up."

It had been a stressful morning and I was relieved to finally be on the plane. I leaned back into the leather airplane seat and sipped the Diet Coke the airline attendant had just brought me, relishing the safety and comfort of first class.

The pilot announced over the loud speaker that the doors were closing and that we would soon be taxying to the runway. That's when I overheard the woman across the aisle from me talking to the passenger in front of her.

"Terry Waite is supposed to be on this flight," she said, pointing to the empty seat beside her. "I flew in with him from London and he said he would be returning on this flight. I wonder where he is."

My thoughts immediately jumped to that conversation on the balcony and the words of my guard as he looked down at Waite and told me that he wasn't doing any negotiating. I thought about the sudden rush to get me out of the country a day early and about the grenades covering the floor of the car.

Though I had no proof that Waite was in danger, my gut was telling me otherwise. I spent most of the five-hour flight to London staring at the empty seat across from me, hoping my worry was unfounded.

I rushed off the plane as soon as it landed, caught a taxi to the office of the English solicitor for Friends in the West, and asked him to assist me in drafting a letter to the Church of England. Then I hand-delivered it to Lambeth Palace, the residence of the Archbishop of Canterbury.

"I'm concerned for the welfare of Terry Waite," my letter read. "You need to get him out of Lebanon immediately. I think he's in danger and could be taken hostage."

My Childhood

...

1

1942

MY CHILDHOOD WAS A jigsaw puzzle riddled with missing pieces. And as early as six, I was desperate to find those pieces and put that puzzle together.

It was 1942 and World War II was raging strong and hard throughout Northern Ireland. Mickey Mouse gas masks, taped-up windows, bomber planes and nightly blackouts were part of my everyday life—as was my anxiety.

Sometimes it scurried throughout my body like ants. Other times, it shot through me like a volt of electricity. It wasn't just the uncertainty of the war erupting around me that made my stomach clench. It was the gnawing feeling that I didn't belong.

I first sensed it the day my dad, Jimmy Ross, arrived home on leave from the army. I entered our narrow row house and saw him sitting in the parlor with my mom, sisters and a few neighbors, drinking tea.

"Hello Raymond," he said, locking his hazel eyes on me.

My body tingled with nervous excitement as I took in my dad for the first time I could remember. He looked older than the photographs I'd seen, with peppered gray hair, rough leathery skin and gray bristles. He smiled when he saw me, revealing teeth yellowed from years of heavy smoking. Even with his smile, there was a hardness about him that made me uneasy.

I pushed my legs toward my dad and offered him a quick hug. Then I took a seat on our linoleum floor and listened to the chatter around me.

The air buzzed with energy. We never knew when loved ones would obtain a leave from the army, so their arrival always felt like Christmas. And like Christmas, they usually always brought gifts.

After a few minutes that seemed to stretch for hours, my dad reached in his army bag and pulled out two red moneyboxes that replicated the post office mailboxes scattered throughout town.

"Here," he said, checking them over before handing one to me and one to my five-year-old sister, Kathleen.

I thought I was going to erupt with joy as I raced upstairs with my sister to examine our gifts. We sat our moneyboxes side by side to compare them. I saw that my moneybox was slightly larger than hers, which made sense to me because I was a year older. But when I picked up her moneybox, I noticed it was much heavier than mine. And when I moved it, I could hear the mass of coins shifting inside.

I was hurt. In my six-year-old mind, Kathleen's coin-filled moneybox confirmed what I was starting to suspect: that my sister was loved more than me.

I didn't have a close relationship with my dad. He served in World War II until I was seven, and even after being discharged early because he'd been gassed in the first World War and left with only one lung, he spent long hours away from home, picking up any odd job he could find to help support our family.

My dad was an honest, hardworking, rough man with a short fuse and a violent temper. I knew his mom had died when he was young, leaving him to be raised by a cruel stepmother who beat into him that beating kids was the way to dole out discipline. But it didn't ease the stinging pain of the hits he delivered by hand or his black leather belt and I steered clear of him as much as possible.

My mother, on the other hand, was the center of my world. She had the kindest eyes, warmest smile and biggest heart I knew. By the time I was six, Lavina Ross was in her early forties, with graying hair and a sturdy rounded frame that was usually covered by the pinny she wore for cooking and cleaning. My mom was like the mother of mothers that everyone came to for advice or help—maybe because being a caregiver was the only thing she knew.

Her own mother died when she was only ten years old, forcing her to drop out of school and step into the role of cook, mother and house cleaner for her seven younger siblings and father. Then she got married and soon had a large family of her own.

Though my oldest three siblings—Willie, Bertie and Viney— were off at war or working in the munitions factory in England, that still left my sister, Netta, my brother Ernie, me, and my sister Kathleen to care for—along with her ailing father, who lived in a two-room shack a short distance away on Dunlop Street. Yet my mother always found the time to listen to me and comfort me. When I was by her side, the sense that I didn't belong vanished. I felt confident and loved and was willing to do anything to protect her and make her happy. But what I was learning about my jigsaw puzzle life was that some missing pieces left holes of sadness that were too big to be filled.

The day I would do anything to erase started with a dream that was so vivid I immediately raced to the scullery to tell my mother.

"What is it, Raymond?" she asked, her face breaking into a warm smile as she took in my excitement.

"I dreamt we received a telegram," I told her. "But it didn't come in a regular yellow envelope. It came in a checkered envelope."

I don't know why I was so excited about my dream. Maybe it was because of the checkered envelope, which I knew was rare and meant that the telegram was important.

My mother didn't say much about it. But when I returned home from school that afternoon, she was holding a telegram that had arrived in the same black-and-white checkered envelope I had dreamed about.

Her face was red and swollen, and there was so much pain in her eyes it hurt to look at her.

"It's from the war office," she managed. "It says that Willie is missing in action somewhere in Burma, and that he's presumed dead."

For a minute I was too stunned to think. I just kept looking at my mother, her grief slamming into me as her news screamed over and over in my mind.

The checkered telegram was from the war office. Willie was missing in action. Willie was presumed dead.

My thoughts jumped back a year, to the last memory I had of my brother. Willie had just gotten married to a French girl he had met in England while training for the war, and was home on a short leave for his honeymoon.

It was late summer just before I started first grade, and one morning he greeted me with a surprise.

"Aida and I are heading to Portrush for the day," he said. "Would you like to come along?"

I was on cloud nine. The north coast wasn't very far from Coleraine—only a twenty-five minute ride by bus. But we rarely went and it was like entering another world. I spent the morning running along the pier and exploring the beach, taking in the sights of the fishing boats, the smell of the salty air and ocean water, and the sounds of the seagulls and waves crashing against the rocks.

Afterward, Willie and Aida bought me fish and chips and treated me to a few rides at the amusement park. Then the magical day was over and soon Willie was gone, headed back to his regiment and deployment.

A surge of fear and guilt rushed through my seven-year-old body as I took in my mother's pain. Then rage took over. The idea that my dream had come true and was causing her so much sadness was more than I could stand.

"What good was that dream, then?" I asked.

My mother moved beside me and wrapped her arms around me.

"It was a warning from God," she answered softly, trying to comfort me despite her pain. "He was trying to prepare me."

Willie was on her mind constantly after that. Aida had given birth to a baby girl, Alma, who now stayed with us while she was in England working in the munitions factory. As my mother held Alma, she talked about Willie and about her hope that he would somehow be found alive and return home to her.

She clung to whatever memories and stories she had of him. My brother Bertie had been the last one to see him. His ship, the HMS Revenge, had pulled into port in Bombay, India and Willie happened to be on the dock, waiting to be transported to Burma.

Willie recognized the ship as the one Bertie was on and the two of them were given a forty-eight hour leave together.

"It's a miracle that they ran into each other half way around the world," my mother said whenever she told the story. "Who's to say that another miracle can't happen?"

I knew her heart was breaking. She tried to hide her sadness, but it came out in the evenings during the BBC news hour. Every night when Big Ben struck nine, we all gathered around the radio to listen to the BBC as it reported news about the war. It was the only way for us to get information about what was happening and what it might mean for our loved ones. Interspersed with the news reports were sad songs and I would watch the tears well in my mother's eyes whenever the song I'll Take You Home Again Kathleen was sung.

It crushed me to see her hurting. Beyond the loss and mystery surrounding Willie's disappearance, my mother constantly worried about money.

There was never enough to go around and she was always choosing between food and bills. A few weeks after the telegram arrived, the rent man knocked on our door and she went into a panic.

"Raymond," she frantically whispered before running off to hide. "Answer the door and tell him I'm not here."

I did as she directed me to, but when the rent man asked me where she was, I answered in the only way I knew how.

"She's hiding in the coal closet," I explained.

With that, the man pushed past me, stormed to our coal closet, swung it open and found her huddled inside.

"You ought to be ashamed of yourself!" I heard him berating her. "Is that what you want to teach that young boy? To lie?"

I wanted to scream at him, tell him to leave her alone; that it wasn't her fault that she didn't have any money to pay the rent. Instead I bit my lip, swallowed my anger and vowed to do whatever I could to bring in some money so my mother would never have to endure such humiliation again.

I started searching out work wherever I could. I collected empty syrup cans I found rummaging through trash bins and sold them to painters for a penny each. When blackberries were in season, I picked buckets of them and sold them to women in our neighborhood to use for jam. By the time I turned eight, I had my first official job as a messenger boy. From there I moved onto a newspaper route that I delivered every morning before school—always turning over everything I earned to my mother.

I also began hunting for food to supplement the strict wartime food rations.

We each had our ration book of coupons that I'd take to Sam Gouth's grocery shop, about a ten-minute walk from our house, to pick up our individual allotment of two ounces of tea, four ounces of sugar and a small ration of butter for the week. Meat and eggs were particularly scarce. So, when I found eggs in a hayloft while picking potatoes at a nearby farm, I snuck a couple and took them home to my mother.

Not long after, while exploring the bulrushes along the River Bann that separated our poor working-class neighborhood of Killowen from the rest of Coleraine, I came across a swan's nest. I knew swans were dangerous and that I could get hurt if the mother swan saw me get near the nest. But that nest held several of the biggest eggs I'd ever seen and I was determined to get one for my mother. Somehow I managed to sneak up to the nest, grab an egg and run before the mother swan knew what I had done. But when I presented the egg to my family, their reaction was anything but joy.

"Raymond, what did you do?" my mother asked, her face turning white "Swans are the King's birds and are protected by the Crown. That was illegal to take. And beyond that, you could have gotten yourself hurt. Did you not know that a swan can break your arm with its wing?"

My stomach was growling for that egg, which I could already taste. But I was also growing hot with shame. I had tried to do something good for my family. Instead I had done something horribly wrong.

Bertie, who was home from the navy, grabbed the egg from me, took it to the outhouse and flushed it down the toilet. Luckily for me, my father wasn't home at the time—which saved me a severe beating.

As the war dragged on, the intensity increased. The Americans had entered the fight and now occupied the north coast—guarding the port from German bombers. They also used the area for training and often scaled the rocky white cliffs to prepare for their invasion in Normandy. The worst of the fighting was in Belfast, a ninety-minute train ride from Coleraine. Bombs hit the city daily, and each week trucks loaded with desperate women and children fleeing the danger arrived in Killowen in search of families that would take them in.

American soldiers also filled the streets throughout my neighborhood. I liked them because they always smiled and waved when I passed them, and not long after they arrived, they held a party for my school class at our church.

My eyes lit up when I saw the cakes and pastries lining the table. These kinds of desserts were a luxury we never had at home and I immediately grabbed one of the pastries and shoved it into my coat pocket.

"What are you doing, son?"

I turned to see a sergeant staring down at me. I couldn't tell by his face if he was angry or curious.

"Well it's mine, isn't it?" I responded defensively. "I'm bringing it home to my mother because she doesn't get anything like this."

The sergeant just looked at me for a minute and then shook his head.

"Never mind that," he said. "You eat that cake, son."

I did as I was ordered, savoring the sugar and pastry dough as it melted in my mouth. Later, when I was getting ready to leave, the sergeant was back. He was holding a box filled with a dozen beautifully assorted cakes and pastries.

"Here," he said. "I want you to take this to your mother."

I loved the Americans after that.

⟡

Some of the kids in my neighborhood viewed school as an escape from the war and stresses of home life. But school was anything but a break for me.

By the time I landed in grade one, it had become so difficult that I did everything I could to avoid going.

We were learning how to write but my handwriting was horrible and no matter how hard I tried, my letters often came out backward. We were also learning how to add and subtract numbers and though I could calculate the equations in my head just fine, I couldn't make sense of the numbers once they were written down on paper.

I counted the minutes until school was over each day and then procrastinated on homework until after dinner because I knew I couldn't do the work. Then it was back to the punishment of school.

"Raymond!" Mrs. Kitty McCelland's voice would thunder from the front of the class. "Where is your homework?"

I would sit unresponsive in my chair and brace myself for what I knew was coming—a painful whack across my back with the cane.

At first my teacher thought I was lazy. But after a while, her beatings became less frequent. That's when I knew she thought I was too stupid to help and had given up on me.

Inside I didn't feel stupid. Though I couldn't seem to write my letters correctly, I was learning how to read—which I loved. But if everybody else thought I was stupid, I didn't know what was going to become of me when I grew up. And even at the age of eight, that worried me.

I was so worried that I decided to bring it up with my mother, figuring she would have a plan for me.

"What do rich people do with their stupid children?" I asked her one evening while she scrubbed laundry on the washboard.

I don't know if she realized how serious I was, but her answer lodged deep in my mind.

"They try to get them into the church or banking," she replied. "Those are the easiest professions."

I struggled so much in school that I was held back a year and had to repeat second grade.

I felt out of place and alone.

It wasn't just my inability to do the schoolwork that set me apart from the others. My mother told me I was a premature baby—only three and a half pounds at birth—and hadn't even been expected to survive. I had managed to defy the odds and live but I was so small and uncoordinated that I couldn't play soccer, the obsession of all of my friends and classmates. So after school, while all the neighborhood boys gathered for their daily afternoon game, I began conjuring my own ways to entertain myself.

I loved comic books—in particular The Beano, which featured an Ostrich called Big Eggo and a story line about a locksmith. The idea that keys could open doors and unlock mysteries fascinated me and I started obsessively hunting for my own keys.

My dad worked as a garbage collector at the time and was always bringing home keys he found discarded in the dump. He put the keys in his desk drawer and that became my starting point.

Most of the keys were large skeleton keys that worked in several different locks and I began making my way through buildings around Killowen, testing them. That's how I discovered that one of my keys unlocked the door to my primary school. It was the first time I actually wanted to enter that building. Unlocking the door and walking through the hallways when no one was around gave me a sense of power that I had never felt before.

I continued testing my keys on buildings and shops when no one was around and was always excited when I came across one that worked. But the biggest rush came when I discovered that one of my keys opened the red mailbox on our church wall located down the hill from my house. There were so many envelopes in that box, just waiting to be delivered to the main post office in town, and I decided I was going to help out.

I went home, grabbed a large paper bag and returned to the mailbox. Then I opened it, carefully scooped the envelopes into the bag and began the mile walk to the Coleraine post office.

I felt important as I carried my paper bag full of mail. The way I saw it, I was helping my neighbors out by getting their letters delivered faster. But as I started emptying my paper bag full of envelopes into the post office mailbox, my brother Bertie appeared beside me.

"Raymond! What do you think you're doing?"

I could hear the sharp rebuke in his voice and it stung.

"I was just trying to help," I answered defensively.

Bertie was fifteen years older than me and was my favorite sibling. He always went out of his way to be kind to me and I wanted to make him proud.

"Do you realize that mail is protected by the Crown, making it the King's mail?" Bertie continued, his tone scolding and berating. "If you got caught, you could go to jail."

I was so crushed by his words it was hard to breathe. I was also scared. Was he serious? Could I really go to jail?

Bertie must have sensed my devastation because when he spoke again, the sharp edge had left his voice.

"Look Raymond, I saw you open that mailbox from the top of the hill and followed you to see what you would do," he said. "I know you didn't mean anything by this and that you were only trying to assist the postman. But no one is going to believe that you took that mail with the intent of re-mailing it. What you've done is illegal and if Dad finds out, he's going to murder you."

The mention of my dad was all I needed to hear. I quickly handed over my stash of keys as Bertie demanded, willing to do anything to avoid Dad's wrath.

I began escaping through books. I spent every spare minute I had consuming mystery and thriller novels, and was deep into a story about a bomber pilot one Saturday morning when Bertie stopped by my bedroom door and invited me to go on a walk with him.

The mail incident was long forgotten by now and Bertie had continued to be my mentor and friend. I quickly pulled on my shoes and jacket, excited to spend time with him.

We walked for a few minutes in comfortable silence. Then Bertie abruptly stopped and turned to me.

"I've got to talk with you about something important," he said, eyeing me intently.

I could hear the seriousness in his voice and sensed that he was about to confide something big.

"Look Raymond," he continued, his eyes still locked on mine, "Great Aunt Mary called our mother over last night. She's dying and told her that one of her final wishes is for you to be told who you are."

My eleven-year-old mind froze. My gut tightened as I braced myself for what I knew deep down was coming.

"It makes no difference to us, Raymond. You're a part of our family. But you weren't born in this family. Ma didn't have the heart to tell you so she asked me to do it."

A jolt of electricity shot through me. My entire body was buzzing and my head was spinning as I tried to process the information Bertie was giving me.

Over the years I'd had plenty of hints that I was different from the rest of my family. It wasn't just the sense that my sister was favored over me, or noticing that I was small with fine features while the rest of my family was a little more stocky and tall. It was also the way the "Aunties" in the neighborhood treated me whenever they saw me.

One woman we all called Aunt Maud always gave me a six pence when our paths crossed at Sam Gouth's grocery store. Another "Aunt," Aunt Maggie, who my dad sometimes took me to visit, often presented me with wool socks she had knitted especially for me.

Great Aunt Mary, the old woman who Bertie said had summoned my mother from her deathbed, always sat in her rocking chair in front of her cottage that overlooked the River Bann. Whenever I passed by, she called me over and gave me three pence.

I found it odd that these women never gave my siblings money or socks. But that was nothing compared to the remarks people made.

Once, angry with a neighbor girl for ratting on me over something small I had done, I had called her Big Eggo, the name of the gaping ostrich in my comic book.

It was the meanest insult I could come up with. But it paled in comparison to the poison she flung back at me.

"They aren't even your family you know," she screamed after me as I ran down the street. "They just took you in because they felt sorry for you."

Another time, while walking home from Sam Gouth's grocery shop, I ran into another girl from my street who began walking with me toward my house.

"So how are the Rosses treating you?" she had asked me. "Are they good to you?"

Even my mother had once alluded to it after I'd done something to upset her.

"If I hadn't taken you in they would have thrown you out the window and over the cliffs into the sea," she had exclaimed in frustration.

At the time I thought she was joking. But over the years I had added the clues together and knew something was up.

Bertie concluded his talk with a final piece of news.

"Your real mother loved you and planned to return for you," he said. "But she was killed in the London blitz."

In some ways, the news Bertie delivered was a comfort to me because it finally solved one of the mysteries I'd been struggling with for years. And learning that my real mother loved me and planned to come back for me was a relief. But now a million more questions were racing through my mind.

Who was my mother?

What did she look like?

What was she like?

Where was her family?

Why did she leave me with the Rosses in the first place?

I didn't ask Bertie any questions because I wasn't comfortable talking about hard things. The only person I ever opened up to was my mother, but I knew I could never ask her the questions I now needed answered. If it was too painful for her to tell me the truth about who I was, there was no way I was going to cause her more pain by asking questions about my birth mother and making her think I was being disloyal to her.

My head felt like it was going to explode. I needed to be alone so I could think and come up with a plan.

Bertie assured me that my life would stay the same. But inside, I knew everything had changed. I loved my mother, Lavina Ross, as fiercely as ever. But I was now consumed with a single quest: to find out everything I could about my birth mother, and figure out who I really was.

2

1949

I AWOKE ABRUPTLY, STARTLED AND confused.

I could feel a hand grabbing me in the dark; hear heavy, stifled breaths. I shook my head, desperate to escape my nightmare. Then reality slammed into me: My drill sergeant—the one who had insisted I move into the barracks next to him for safety from the older cadets—was in my bed, pressing his body against me.

I could hear the voice screaming in my head; pleading for someone to help. But when I opened my mouth, no sound came out. My vocal chords were paralyzed.

It was the summer of 1949—three months before my thirteenth birthday—and I was at a sprawling military camp about an hour from home, undergoing a week-long cadet training exercise that culminated with a trip to Belfast to experience a parade featuring members of the royal family.

Joining the cadets was an idea that had hit me a few months earlier, while walking past the cadet training facility in Coleraine on my way to my new intermediate school. I was looking for something fun to do and the cadets—with their uniforms and rifle drills—sounded like the perfect answer.

All of the other cadets were older than me and attended an elite boarding school in town. I knew they viewed me as a fragile street kid from the wrong side of the river. But I didn't care. I was focused on becoming a top cadet.

I was excited as I settled into my new living quarters earlier that evening. Unlike the other barracks, which was packed with twenty rowdy boys who picked fistfights and urinated in each other's boots, the barracks the sergeant had moved me to was a large open room with a bed on either side, providing plenty of privacy and space for me and the other boy who had been singled out.

Now, as I lay frozen in bed, I wondered if that boy could hear what was happening. Could he hear the heavy breathing? Feel my terror?

I bit the inside of my mouth and closed my eyes, trying to shut out the panic and pain. Then it was over and the sergeant was gone.

I reported the assault as soon as morning arrived. But even then, I knew I couldn't go public with the incident. The news that the Ross family was not my real family was still ringing through my mind and I didn't want to do anything to bring them shame or cause problems. Above all, I didn't want people to think I was weak.

I buried the painful secret deep inside, filing it away with my other secret—the secret about my identity. Since Bertie's revelation, I had spent hours holed up in my room, fantasizing about my birth mother and what life might have been like if she had made it back for me before being killed in the blitz.

I imagined a kind, beautiful woman who was rich and lived a glamorous life in England suddenly showing up at our door.

"Raymond," she would say in a soothing voice as she reached for my hand. "I've missed you so much. I'm so sorry that I left you, but I'll never leave you again."

That fantasy would quickly revert back to real life and I'd think about my mother's family—my grandma, my grandpa and possible aunts and uncles. I wondered why they didn't take me in after my mother was killed; why I was left with the Ross family. I had so many questions, but I had no one to go to for answers.

I finished out the week at camp and returned home, determined to block the attack from my mind. Despite the hurt I carried inside me, things were starting to look up.

My family had recently moved into new council housing that had been built to accommodate the surging post-war housing needs for returning war veterans and their new and growing families.

From the minute I stepped foot into our new house, I felt rich. For starters, it had four bedrooms—which meant that I got my own room. It also came with an indoor toilet. But what had me really excited was the bathing room.

"You've got to come look at this!" I shouted to my sister, Kathleen, who was busy exploring other rooms in the house. "It's got the biggest tub you've ever seen!"

In our old house, we cleaned ourselves in a round metal tub that we pulled into the parlor and filled with hot water we heated on our coal-burning stove. Along with the lack of privacy and the fact that it took forever to heat enough water to fill the metal bin, it was much too small to cover our entire bodies. The whole process was an uncomfortable, time-consuming chore that I forced myself to do once a week. Now—with the large built-in tub and hot running water—taking a bath was a luxury that I could enjoy anytime I pleased.

For a twelve-year old boy trying to fit in at school, there was another huge benefit to the new house: it's location. The house was situated across the River Bann in Milburn, a wealthier neighborhood than Killowen—which was known as the poor, rough side of town.

Now when people asked, I could proudly say I lived in Milburn, without mentioning that I lived in one of the fixed-rent council row houses, which would have given it all away.

Life calmed down at the new house. My nineteen-year-old brother, Ernie, who had been in constant trouble with the law, had enrolled in the Royal Ulster Rifles to avoid a six-month jail sentence. Without the heated clashes between him and my dad, there was less tension around home.

I continued to lose myself in mystery and adventure stories, as well as biographies about famous explorers and war heroes. I was drawn to stories about people who overcame adversity and went on to accomplish great things. I read about Florence Nightingale and her impact on nursing during the Crimean War. I read about spitfire pilots and how their courage helped end the war. I also consumed classics such as *Bleak House* by Dickens. I was so captivated by the stories that I sometimes pulled my blanket over my head and the bare light bulb that hung next to my bed and read through the night.

I was also captivated by movies and headed to the theater whenever I could afford it. I loved character-driven films that delivered inspirational messages, and was fascinated by the real stories behind the actors. I knew, for example, that Leslie Howard, who played Ashley Wilkes in *Gone with the Wind*, had served as an MI6 agent and was killed in World War II, and that Jimmy Stewart had been a brigadier general in the air force.

Any remaining time was spent hanging out with my friend Jackie Dinsmore, a boy I'd known since grade school. Sometimes the two of us would head to the movie theater together. Other times we'd make the seven-mile walk to the coast and spend the day at the beach. When we felt like kicking back, we hung out in his family's parlor, where Mrs. Dinsmore always treated us to tea and pastries.

Life felt good for a change. But the pressure to figure out my future was mounting and by the summer of 1950, my anxiety had reached an all-time high.

I was only months away from turning fourteen, which meant I would finally be done with school at the end of my first semester. I could hardly wait for that. But it meant that I needed a plan.

My friends were beginning to line up apprenticeships in plumbing, mechanics or construction; but none of those professions interested me. And with college out of the question given my poor grades and struggle with academics, I didn't know what I could do.

I spent a week taking long walks alone, thinking through my dilemma. Then it hit me: I could become a professional photographer.

I had always been fascinated by photography and geography. In my school, maps and photos of faraway places covered the walls and I would study them, dreaming about exploring those places as an adult.

It was the photos that had drawn me into those places around the world and if I became a photographer, I figured it would give me the chance to see those places for myself. And the best part about photography was that it didn't require writing or math.

Now that I knew what I wanted to do with my life, I didn't want to waste any time getting started. I remembered walking past a photography studio about a twenty-minute walk from my house and immediately set out for my destination.

My plan was simple: I'd get an apprenticeship, learn the trade and eventually become a famous photographer.

I arrived at the door located at the bottom of a row house and nervously climbed the narrow steps to the second floor. I could feel the butterflies in my stomach. But I was on a mission and forced my legs to keep moving.

At the top of the steps was an open door that led to the studio reception area. A pretty woman who looked to be in her early thirties was sweeping the linoleum floor but stopped when she heard me enter.

"Can I help you?" she asked kindly.

"I've come to see if I could get a job," I blurted before I lost my nerve.

She stood there for what seemed like an hour, just looking at me.

"Okay," she said finally.

I took this as a "yes' and quickly grabbed the broom from her hand and began sweeping so she could see what a good decision she'd made.

"No, no, no," the woman said quickly, clearly flustered. "You've got to speak to my husband."

She left me standing with the broom and disappeared behind one of the three doors that stemmed from the reception area. A minute later she was back, accompanied by a man with warm eyes and a friendly smile who also looked to be in his early thirties.

"I'm Jim," he said. "What can I do for you?"

I took a deep breath, trying to calm myself.

"I want to train to become a photographer," I told him, hoping my voice sounded confident. "I want to be your apprentice."

Jim paused and glanced at his wife. They didn't talk but I could see the look of surprise pass between them. Then Jim turned back to me and studied me intently.

"We can't pay you much," he said finally. "But we'll take you on. I'm sure we can figure out something for you to do."

Exhilaration shot through me, though I was careful to maintain a calm outward demeanor. I couldn't believe it. I was really doing it. My future was now solved. I was going to become a professional photographer.

The next day I was back, standing in the dark room watching in the dim light as Jim dipped film into a tub filled with chemicals. As he worked, he carried on a conversation with a friend who had dropped by for a visit.

I was concentrating so hard on watching Jim and trying to memorize the steps involved in processing film that I didn't pay much attention to what they were saying until I heard the words "missionary work" and "David Livingstone."

David Livingstone was a famous Scottish missionary and explorer who had traveled extensively throughout Africa and became known as a dedicated Christian, a courageous explorer, and a fervent anti-slavery advocate. He was a national hero and everyone knew his story because a movie had been made about his life. I knew he was a missionary, but what inspired me were his exploits as an explorer. He lived a life packed with excitement and danger while doing good deeds and making famous discoveries—such as that of Victoria Falls located on the border of Zambia and Zimbabwe. His was the kind of life I dreamed about.

"What do you think about missionaries?" Jim's friend asked, noticing that I was listening in on their conversation.

"I think I might like to be one someday," I replied, my thoughts still locked on David Livingstone.

My answer caught Jim's attention.

"That's great, Raymond," he said. "But you have to be a Christian. Are you a Christian?"

"Of course," I answered.

His question seemed obvious, since as far as I could tell, everyone I knew was a Christian. Like most everyone around me, I had been baptized in the Church of Ireland and had spent nearly every Sunday there since.

Not that I wanted to be there. I found the sermons long and boring and viewed my mandatory church attendance as a weekly prison sentence. Sometimes, for entertainment, my friends and I would arrive early and sprinkle cornflakes on the floors between the pews so we could hear it crunch and see the horrified looks on people's faces when they stepped on it while trying to take a seat.

Jim looked at me quizzically.

"Do you know if you'll go to Heaven when you die, Raymond?"

This question took a little more thought. The last time I'd contemplated death and afterlife was when I was seven and so sick with double pneumonia that the doctor who had come to check on me predicted I wouldn't last through the night.

The thought of dying terrified me and when I managed to defy the doctor's prediction and battle through the worst of my illness, I brought it up with my mother.

"Where would I go if I die?" I asked her, thinking of the caskets and burial plots I had heard an insurance man discussing with my parents during a recent visit to our house.

"You would go to heaven because you haven't reached the age of accountability yet," she had replied.

Her answer back then had comforted me and though I had recently been confirmed and was now responsible for my sins, I had endured enough church lessons and teachings that I felt I had a pretty good handle on what it took to get to heaven.

"Yes," I answered, looking at Jim intently. "If I go to church, am good and honest and try to do my best for people, I think I'll go to heaven."

Jim shook his head.

"No, that isn't the way," he said firmly.

I was confused. But I was also intrigued.

"Well, what is the way then?" I asked.

"You have to be born again," Jim replied.

Now I was really confused. But something had been ignited inside of me. I had overheard Jim talking about his work as a lay preacher and could tell that he and his friend were different from other people I knew. They both radiated peace, confidence and happiness, and I wanted to feel that, too.

"So how do I become born again?" I asked.

Jim removed the film from the chemicals, hung it up to dry and trained his full attention on me.

"You have to understand that God gave his only son, Jesus, to die for you so that your sins could be forgiven and you could have everlasting life," Jim said. "Then you've got to confess your sins and ask the Lord Jesus to come into your heart."

His words were clear and simple. I may have only been thirteen, but the idea that I could just confess my sins directly to God and ask him to come into my heart made sense to me.

But now I had another nagging concern.

"If I ask, how do I know if God will take me?"

Jim smiled.

"It's a promise from God and he can't break his word," he said.

I followed him into the reception area, where he reached into a drawer, pulled out a well-worn Bible and thumbed through it until he found the page and verse he was looking for.

"He that comes to me I will in no wise cast out," Jim read, quoting John 6:37.

Relief washed over me as the scripture sunk in. I had never thought about my faith before and had never been asked to make a decision. I'd gone to church because it's what my family did and what was expected of me. Now I was being presented with a choice that I knew intuitively would change my life: I could decide to have a personal relationship with God by turning my life over to Him and inviting Him into my heart.

I knew I wanted it. And I wanted it now. I had never felt so sure about anything.

As soon as my lunch break arrived, I quickly walked the mile and a half to my house and devoured my sandwich. Then I scaled the stairs to my bedroom, shut the door behind me and got down on my knees to pray.

I knew the Lord's Prayer by heart. But it was just words that I had memorized. I had never thought of it as actually talking to God. Now I was determined to make a connection and have Him hear me.

"Lord, I am a sinner and I want you to forgive my sins and come into my heart and into my life," I said, pausing to make sure God had time to digest my words and understand how sincere I was. "I know that you are going to accept me because you promised if I came, you wouldn't turn me away."

It was a simple prayer. But I felt and meant every word of it and I knew God heard me. As I prayed, peace and calmness washed over me. For the first time in my life, I felt like I belonged.

I couldn't wait to get on with what I now felt was my calling: missionary work. I raced back to the photography studio, where I found Jim and his friend still deep in conversation.

"I think I would like to be a missionary," I interjected as soon as there was a pause.

Jim shot me an exasperated look.

"Yes," he said, trying to keep his voice patient. "But as I just explained to you, Raymond, you have to be a Christian."

"But I *am* a Christian," I replied. "I went home, got on my knees, confessed that I'm a sinner and asked the Lord to come into my heart.

"What else do I need to do?"

Jim just looked at me for a minute without saying a word. Then he shook his head and a huge smile broke open across his face.

"Well," he said finally. "If you believe in your heart—which I can see that you do—than you need to make a public confession.

"Look, Raymond. I'm to preach at Londonderry Guildhall next Sunday. Why don't you come along?"

The words "public confession" knocked the air out of me. But I was so excited to be a Christian and be surrounded by others who had been born again that I was determined to do whatever it took. It wasn't until I was on the forty-mile bus ride to Londonderry with Jim a few days later that the panic set in.

Stage fright didn't come close to defining the crippling fear that took over me when I was asked to speak or perform in front of a crowd. It was as though my body locked up and stopped working. A year earlier, my music teacher was forming a choir and had asked me to take a spot on stage. I was so consumed with nerves that I fainted as soon as I stepped up to the podium.

"Please don't ask me to get up in front of people," I pleaded with Jim as we neared Guildhall, an imposing neo-gothic landmark filled with stained glass windows. "I just can't do it."

I figured Jim understood my plight and would spare me. But midway through his sermon, I heard him say my name.

"There's a young man with me tonight and he's going to come give his testimony," he said, looking directly at me. "Raymond, please come up."

My heart was beating so fast in my chest it sounded like a drum roll. My stomach dropped and I could feel my lunch creeping up my throat.

I sensed everyone's eyes on me, watching to see what I would do.

Every part of me wanted to crawl under my seat and hide. Instead, I forced my legs into a standing position and slowly began making my way to the front of the hall.

My hands were clenched into tight fists to keep them from shaking but I couldn't stop my legs from trembling. The lights of the hall beat down on me, glaring at me. Heat surged through me and I could feel the sweat through my white button-down Sunday shirt.

I made it onto the stage where Jim was waiting. Then the dizziness kicked in, my head got light and everything went dark.

The next thing I remembered was lying on the wood floor, hearing the chatter of concerned voices around me.

I didn't want to open my eyes and face the people. But despite my embarrassment, I was happy. I was a Christian and though I hadn't managed to publicly confess my newfound faith, I had faced my worst fear and had been willing to do whatever it took to show God how committed I was to Him.

I kept my eyes closed for a minute and whispered a prayer in my head.

"Lord. I'm going to share my testimony every time I'm asked," I said silently. "The outcome will be up you."

I was exhausted and ready for sleep by the time I arrived home late that night. But I awoke early the next morning and pulled out the Bible I had been given years before.

I had always viewed scripture reading as a chore and had never considered delving into the Bible on my own. But now I was hungry for the messages and wisdom it contained.

I opened it to the book of Mark and started reading. After a few minutes, I came across the words that would change everything.

All things are possible to him who believes.

I stared at the line—Mark 9:23—and read it again, letting the words sink in.

ALL THINGS ARE POSSIBLE TO HIM WHO BELIEVES.

I knew God had directed me to that passage, and it was all I needed to know. I felt powerful and calm. I could sense God's presence. And I was now convinced that if I put all my faith in God and truly believed, I could do whatever I set out to do.

3

Fall 1950

THE WOMAN'S WORDS CAUGHT me off guard.

"I'm sorry," she said after spending a half hour combing and re-combing through a large file cabinet tucked in
a room adjacent to the reception area. "We don't have a record of a
Raymond Ross born on that day. Are you sure you have the right
date?"

I felt my gut tighten. Of course I had the right date. I had just
celebrated my fourteenth birthday. What's more, September 26,
1936, was the date listed on my Church of Ireland baptismal certificate.

But now the familiar questions surrounding my identity were
swirling in my mind again. I could feel the stress shooting through me
because I needed my birth certificate to get my National Insurance
Card, which was being required by my new employer now that I was
fourteen and officially ready to work.

My photography apprenticeship had ended after only two and
a half months because as much as he wanted to help me out, Jim
couldn't afford to keep me on. I didn't mind because I was now so immersed in my newfound Christian faith that I was convinced I want-

ed to pursue a life in the ministry. But in the meantime, I needed an income. So when I heard about a job at a small country grocery store and petrol station a few miles outside of town, I had quickly applied.

I left the birth certificate office confused and nervous. It had been three years since Bertie revealed that I wasn't biologically born into the family and that my birth mother had died in the Blitz. The topic hadn't come up since and it seemed like such an off-limits subject that I dreaded bringing it up. But if I wanted to work, I needed my birth certificate and I couldn't see another way around it.

As I walked the mile stretch to my house, my mind sifted through the identity puzzle pieces I'd been accumulating—pieces that I continued to push deep down inside me because they were too painful to process. As much as I tried to avoid it, my thoughts jumped to the humiliating encounter I had endured on the bus a few weeks earlier.

Just thinking about it made my face heat up.

I don't know how I had concluded that my mother's cousin—a man we all called "Uncle Bob" when he stopped by our house for occasional visits—was really my dad. Maybe it was because I noticed that he paid closer attention to me than my sister, Kathleen. Whatever the case, I knew it in my gut even before he spotted me and took the seat next to me.

I was headed to the coast to operate a kiosk Jim had set up to service summer tourists interested in having their film developed. I just wanted to enjoy the thirty-minute bus ride in silence and definitely wasn't in the mood for awkward small talk.

Bob asked me the regular questions: how I was doing, what I was up to, and how my mother was, and told me that he was headed to the coast to visit his sister, Annie.

Then his face turned tense and the tone of his voice changed.

"I loved your mother and wanted to marry her," he said. "But she didn't want to marry me."

My head was spinning and I was on fire. I was trapped against a window in a crowded bus and needed to escape.

Bob kept talking, mumbling some excuse about why he had left me with the Rosses. I heard buzzing. Then everything went quiet. I could feel every eye in the crowded bus on me, listening to Bob try to explain why he had given me away.

I was burning with embarrassment. Didn't he know he was making a fool out of both of us? Why couldn't he just stop talking?

I pushed my way off the bus the second it landed at my stop and sprinted to the security of the photo kiosk. But within minutes, Bob was there, insisting I accompany him to his sister's house for tea.

"Just put up the "stepped out" sign," he said when I tried to politely decline by explaining that I couldn't leave the shop unattended. "No one will miss you for a few minutes."

There were so many questions I could have asked this man who I now knew for certain was my biological father. I could tell he was nervous and trying his best to reach out to me and talk through things. But I was too shaken up to think and at the moment, the only questions racing through my mind were ones I knew I could never ask.

"Why," I wanted to ask, "did you choose to leave me with the Ross family when they already had so many kids to care for and were struggling so hard just to get by? "Why choose the poorest family and your cousin to take me in when you had so many sisters who were all better off?"

It wasn't until years later that I would learn that the barber down the street who cut my hair every few months was my grandfather. He never breathed a word to me or gave any indication that he knew me beyond being a customer. But it was that deep, cutting pain of rejection that consumed me as I endured the short walk to Aunt Annie's house—yet another relative who didn't publicly acknowledge who I was—and the awkward twenty minutes of tea before excusing myself and rushing back to the safety of the shop.

I had tried to erase the incident from my mind. But now, as I braced myself for the conversation about my birth certificate with my mother, the pain and humiliation of that day was as fresh as if it had just happened and I wasn't sure I could stand much more.

I arrived home and somehow managed to push the words about my missing birth certificate out of my mouth. My mother didn't get upset, as I feared she would. Instead, she headed to my father's desk and rummaged through some papers. Then she was back, pushing a document into my hands.

"You see, Raymond, we never officially adopted you because your mother was going to come back for you," she explained before I had a chance to look at the paper. "So instead, we had a legal guardianship drawn up."

Her words knocked the air out of me. I had wanted answers for so long, but now that they were coming, I wasn't sure I was ready. What did she mean I wasn't formally adopted? Had the Rosses felt obligated to take me in and become my legal guardian?

I forced the thoughts out of my mind as my eyes quickly scanned the legal guardianship document. Near the bottom of the page I found the words I had been searching for—the name Margaret Barnett. And directly beneath my birth mother's name was my birth name: Robert Raymond Barnett.

I stared at the paper; trying to process the information I had wanted so desperately—information that had been hidden in a drawer in my house for fourteen years.

"Would you like to see a picture of her?" my mother asked, interrupting my thoughts.

She went back to the desk and returned with an old black-and-white photo. I was a baby—no more than a month old—and was being held by a woman who was dressed in a long dark coat. She looked to be in her early twenties and was as beautiful as the mother I had fantasized about. She was a classic beauty with dark, long hair, almond shaped eyes, high cheekbones and smooth creamy skin. I studied her face, wondering what she was thinking the day that picture was taken, and what life would have been like if she hadn't died.

"She sent clothes for you when you were a baby," my mother continued. "She definitely planned to come back for you and would have if she hadn't been killed in the Blitz."

So many emotions were swirling inside me that I couldn't feel any of them. The only anchor my mind could latch onto was the practical problems that now awaited me: I had to figure out how to get this paperwork mess resolved so I could get my National Insurance Card. And then I had to explain to my new boss that I wasn't really Raymond Ross.

I headed back to the birth certificate office with my new documentation.

If the woman who was helping me was taken back by my situation, she didn't indicate it. She was kind and matter-of-fact when she spoke.

"Well son, what name do you want to be called?"

I hadn't had time to think that through. But as I contemplated her question, I realized there was only one logical choice.

"Well I guess I have to go with whatever my legal name is," I responded.

"Are you sure?" the woman asked.

I wouldn't have done anything to hurt my mother, Lavina Ross. But now that I knew my real last name and was one step closer to figuring out who I was, I had to claim it for my own.

"I'm sure," I replied.

I left the government office with a National Insurance Card that read Raymond Barnett. I didn't tell my mother that I had changed my last name, and I never mentioned it to my friends. I just became someone new.

The mystery over my identity ate away at me and might have done me in had it not been for my newfound faith and the powerful post-war evangelical wave that was sweeping through England and Northern Ireland.

The Youth for Christ movement, started by Billy Graham in the United States, had caught fire throughout the United Kingdom. Teams of youth outreach ministers arrived in Northern Ireland, and every Saturday night, a Youth for Christ meet up was held in a large hall in the center of town.

Christian teenagers flocked to the weekly events. Unlike the long, boring church sermons I had grown up with, these Youth for Christ events featured popular music and short, inspiring sermons that spoke to our generation.

I headed there alone on my Saturday nights and eventually made friends with other Christian teens from town. But I held out hope that my core group of friends—Jackie, his older brother, Billy, and other guys we hung out with—would also decide to invite Jesus into their hearts and discover the peace and joy I had found.

I thought about the two things in my life that seemed most impossible: my friends choosing to turn their life over to God, and me overcoming my fear of public speaking. Then I made a list of twenty-five friends and began praying individually for each of them to invite God into their hearts and life. I also asked the Lord to help me get over my fear of public speaking—all while holding onto the promise I'd read in the Book of Mark: *All things are possible to him who believes.*

Soon my anxiety over public speaking was gone. I even began to enjoy it. And within a year and a half of my decision to invite Christ into my heart and life, Jackie, Billy and a few other friends had made the decision as well. Over the course of time, every one of those twenty-five friends I had prayed for became believers.

My friends and I started attending the evangelical crusades that would occasionally come to Coleraine and even began preaching on street corners to whoever would listen. After a while, we decided we wanted to start a church of our own in an old unused hall in Killowen. We pulled together our money for rent and secured permission to start the church. Soon we had a thriving youth ministry that included Bible study on Tuesday nights, prayer meetings on Thursday nights and church services on Sunday nights.

Aside from being star athletes, nice-looking and charismatic, Jackie and his brothers were talented musicians and took charge of the music. I handled the sermons. Before long, word was out and Christian youth from the better side of Coleraine began making the trek across the river each Sunday evening, anxious to attend the church run by other Christian youth.

Between our youth ministry and the full-time job I had recently landed at a laundry in town, I was so busy that I wasn't home much. But when I was, I could feel the heaviness and sadness that continued to burden my mother.

Shortly after joining the Royal Ulster Rifles, Ernie's platoon was deployed to Korea and he had gone missing in action. His command-ing officer had written a letter explaining that Ernie had been on rear guard when the platoon was attacked and hadn't made it out with the rest of his unit.

We didn't know whether Ernie had been killed or was a prisoner of war and my mother was now holding vigil for two sons—though it was early 1952 we all knew in our hearts that Willie was gone.

Sometimes we gathered in the parlor after dinner with Willie's wife, Aida, and Jean—the woman Ernie had married prior to his de-ployment—to share stories and reminisce. That's what we were doing one Friday evening in early spring when I discovered the thick propa-ganda catalog that had arrived in the mail from the Communist Party of the United Kingdom. While the others talked, I took a seat on the floor near the fire and began flipping through the thick catalog, look-ing at the pictures taken at prisoner-of-war camps throughout North Korea. The pages showed images of happy captives playing football and having fun, and were full of flowery words about how well they were being treated. No one believed any of it and considered the catalog junk. But I was intrigued because in small captions beneath each of the hundreds of group pictures were the first initials and last names of the prisoners featured in that picture.

I don't know what clicked inside me. But something told me that the catalog held the answer to Ernie's disappearance and I was determined to get to the bottom of it. The type was so small that I retrieved a magnifying glass from my bedroom and began combing through the catalog page by page, tediously reading through each name listed under the photos. I was about an hour into my research when I came across the entry I had been hoping for: E. Ross.

My heart jumped as I read the initial and last name. I quickly scanned the group photo above the name, studying each face before coming across one that looked a lot like my brother.

I held my magnifying glass up to the grainy photo, trying to get a good look at the soldier's face. There were at least forty men in the black and white picture so the faces were hard to make out. But after studying the image carefully, I was convinced it was Ernie.

I spent the next few minutes going back and forth between the name E. Ross and the face in that group photo. Once I was certain it was him, I waited for a break in the conversation and then made my pronouncement.

"Well," I said, glancing around the room, "it looks like our Ernie is alive."

First everyone went quiet. Then there was an eruption of chatter.

"What are you talking about?" my dad asked in a booming voice that drowned out the others.

"I found him," I replied, feeling pride wash over me. "He's right here in this catalog."

All at once eight hands were grabbing for the magazine. Soon Ernie's wife was crying and everyone was hugging and cheering. I felt a quiet sense of satisfaction as my dad placed the call to the army to report the news. I was proud that I had done something important to contribute. But what mattered most was seeing my mother's face light up and knowing that I had brought her happiness.

I WAS AT WORK a few months later, marking and tagging clothes for cleaning, when I came across a deep purple dress. It was a form-fitting dress made of shimmery, expensive-looking material and was so beautiful that I checked the label to see where it was from.

When I saw the word London, my heart skipped a beat and my thoughts immediately jumped to my birth mother. I had memorized the one picture I now had of her and could visualize her in this dress. It just seemed like the kind of classic, beautiful dress she would have worn.

That same inner voice that drove me to comb through the communist party catalog looking for Ernie kicked in again. I grabbed the file of index cards and started flipping through them until I found the number on the card that matched the one assigned to the dress. There, in front of me, was the information I somehow knew I would find. The dress was registered under the name Barnett with a delivery address of Culmore Point, which is where I had been told my birth mother's parents lived.

I stared at that card for what seemed like hours, trying to process this newest bit of information. Then my mind started racing and jumping from one far-flung conclusion to the next.

This dress came from London, the last known place where my birth mother lived. So, it had to belong to her. And if that was the case, it meant only one thing: she was alive.

My mind kept racing. If my mother's dress was here, it must mean that she was visiting her family on Culmore Point and had decided to get her dress cleaned while in town. It could even mean that she had moved back to Culmore Point and was living only a forty-minute train ride away.

I knew that my conclusions were highly improbable and that I could be getting my hopes up for nothing. But I also knew it wasn't an accident that I had been guided to look at the index card. I knew God was directing me and something inside me told me this dress was another big clue to my identity.

I caught a train to Londonderry on my first day off, determined to find out the truth. I had spent hours mulling the situation over in my mind and had concocted a story that I figured would get them to tell me what I needed to know without causing any problems or triggering an alarm.

It was late afternoon by the time my train landed in Londonderry and rain was already beginning to fall. My stomach cramped with anxiety as I thought about the plan I had laid out, which now sounded ridiculous.

How was I going to do this? How was I going to work up the courage to knock on that door? And how was I going to actually convince them to give me the information?

I pulled my hood tight over my head to block out the rain and began the three or four mile trek to Culmore Point that I had mapped out the day before. I crossed a large bridge and then followed the road that lined the River Foyle. I passed a string of residential houses and kept walking until I reached Culmore Point. There, situated on a spit of land, was an ancient stone tower that everyone called Culmore Castle.

The narrow tower dated back to the 1600s and looked medieval. I stood staring at the tower for several minutes, too terrified to move. Then I whispered a prayer, willed my legs to carry me to the heavy wooden door, and knocked.

When it opened, I found myself looking at an elderly woman donning an old-fashioned bonnet. I could tell by the way she gazed at me that she could hardly see.

"Can I help you?" she asked, staring past me.

"I'm here because my mother, Lavina Ross, was a good friend of Margaret Barnett," I blurted, launching into my story before I lost my nerve. "She lost touch with her during the war and since I was passing through Londonderry, I thought I would stop by and see if I could find out where Margaret is living today so I could surprise her."

The old woman looked perplexed. "Is everything okay with Margaret?" she asked.

My heart was beating so hard it felt like it was going to beat out of my chest.

"Oh I'm sure she's fine," I replied quickly. "My mother just lost touch so I'm just trying to locate her."

The old woman seemed confused.

"My son, Harry, will be home soon and can help you," she said. "You are welcome to come in and wait."

I followed the old woman into the stone tower and took a seat next to the open, coal-burning fireplace to wait for her son to arrive. I concentrated on projecting calm and quiet. But inside I was so amped up I was ready to explode. If I understood the old lady's comments correctly, my hunch was right: my birth mother was actually *alive*. One thing for certain was that I was sitting two feet from my grandmother and was about to meet my uncle.

It was dark and raining outside by the time Harry walked through the door. I was ready to burst and couldn't carry on the charade any longer.

I told him I had to get going and asked if he could direct me to the bus. He followed me outside. That's when I let the truth come out.

"It's my understanding that Margaret is my mother and I was told she was killed in the London Blitz," I said, locking my eyes on his and concentrating to keep my voice steady and strong. "But I know that's not true so I'm trying to find out where she is."

I'm sure Harry was shocked. But he must have known about my existence because he didn't flinch and he didn't protest. He told me my mother had been in a building that was bombed but had survived the attack and was still living in London. He said her married name was Mrs. Charles Martin. Then he recited her address while I scribbled it with a shaking hand into a small notebook I had carried with me.

I was so taken back by Harry's revelation I was having a hard time absorbing the information. He had just confirmed that everything I had been told for years was a lie. My birth mother didn't die. She was alive and well.

"What are you going to do?" he asked as he walked me to a nearby bus stop that would take me back to the train station.

I shook my head, still trying to grasp the news.

"I don't know."

I was swimming in such a tidal wave of emotions it was hard to keep my head above water.

I was thrilled that my mother was alive and proud of myself for unraveling the mystery that had consumed me for so many years. I was also stinging from the knowledge that my birth mother had been alive all these years and had never once reached out to me.

I spent the train ride thinking it through and decided there must be a good reason my mother hadn't come back for me.

By the time my train pulled into the station in Coleraine, I knew there was only one thing to do next: go to London to meet her and find out from her what really happened.

4

Summer 1953

I WAS TOO WOUND UP to sleep during the overnight boat ride from Belfast to Heysham, a port town in Northern England. Instead I paced the deck of the boat, my thoughts racing from one possibility to the next as I listened to the waves crash against the bow. I stared into the dark sea, fantasizing about the new life that awaited me in London—a life that I was convinced would include a relationship with my birth mother.

I didn't tell anyone about my plan to finally meet and reunite with my birth mother. Aside from her brother, Harry, no one even knew that I knew she was alive. Instead, I told my mother and friends a partial truth—that I was moving to London to pursue a job in the ministry.

Like other Irish mothers, my mother had encouraged me to move to England to seek a better life for myself and she was proud that I was taking charge of my future. I was only sixteen, younger than most of the youth who headed for London, but she believed in me.

"Raymond, you need to move away from here if you want to make something of yourself," she had repeatedly advised me. "The opportunities are in London. That's where you need to go."

It was early Sunday afternoon by the time I docked in Heysham, boarded the boat train to London and landed at Euston Station. I had only a suitcase full of clothes and a five-pound note to my name and knew I needed to find a job fast if I was going to survive. But I pushed that thought to the back of my mind and concentrated on my immediate task: finding a place to sleep for the night.

I headed down the central London street, exhilarated by the swarm of people around me. I took in the soaring buildings, surprised by how many of them were still in ruins though nearly eight years had passed since the end of the war.

After walking a few blocks, I saw a sign advertising a bed and breakfast for two and a half pounds and turned over half of my money to secure a room for the night. Then I took a seat in the drawing room, poured myself a cup of tea and sat back to soak in my accomplishment and contemplate my next move.

"Are you traveling through here?" I heard an American voice ask. The voice belonged to a university student who was in England on holidays.

We began talking, swapping information about ourselves, sharing our dreams and the excitement of being in London on our own.

"Hey, I'm headed to Hyde Park Corner," he said after a few minutes of conversation. "Do you want to come?"

I hadn't slept since leaving Coleraine nearly twenty-four hours earlier and could feel the exhaustion worming its way through my body. But I wasn't about to miss an invitation to check out Hyde Park Corner on a Sunday afternoon.

Hyde Park Corner was famous for its speakers and performers. Anyone could take the stage there on Sunday afternoons and throngs of locals and tourists alike headed there to take it in.

I could feel the energy charge in the air as we followed Oxford Street to the park. Heckles and cheers could be heard from as far as two blocks away. There were speakers pushing the Labor movement, gospel preachers, activists, jugglers and musicians.

I milled through the crowds, taking in the sights and sounds but mostly just soaking up the experience and excitement of the moment.

I was really doing it. I was in London, the center of the world, ready to make it on my own, connect with my birth mother and begin a new chapter of my life.

I awoke the next morning rested and determined. After purchasing a sandwich for dinner, I was down to two pounds and thirty shillings, not enough to pay for another night's stay. I had roughly twelve hours to find a job and a place to sleep for the night. But I wasn't scared by the thought; I was excited.

I enjoyed the complimentary English breakfast in the drawing room; savoring the few minutes of relaxation it afforded me. Then I checked out of the bed and breakfast, grabbed my suitcase and followed the cement walkway, moving aimlessly in whatever direction my legs took me as I tried to devise a plan. After a mile or so, I decided to head toward Westminster Abbey.

I'm not sure what drew me to the historic church. But instead of going in as I had planned to do, I looked across the street and saw that I was standing in front of Methodist Central Hall, the UK headquarters for the Methodist Church.

My friends and I were so passionate about our newfound faith that we sought out inspirational sermons wherever we could find them and had struck up a friendship with Reverend D. Hall Ludlow at the Methodist Church in Coleraine. He was impressed that a group of teenage boys were such devoted Christians and had recently asked me to teach the children's story during the morning service.

I had heard about Methodist Central Hall and decided to check it out. It was a Monday so I wasn't sure that anyone would even be there. But I figured it was worth a shot because if people were around, it was possible they had a few ideas for me and could point me in the right direction.

The imposing brick building took up the entire city block and looked more like an office building than a church, though the dome sitting on the roof gave it away.

I entered through a side door and found myself in a small reception area.

"Can I help you?" a girl behind the counter asked. She didn't look much older than me, maybe nineteen or twenty, and offered a warm, friendly smile when she saw me.

"Yes, I hope so," I started. "I want to become a minister and have just landed in London so I stopped in to see what I could find out."

The girl looked from me, to my suitcase, and then back at me.

"Well," she replied, "It's very interesting timing because the executive leadership of the church is having a meeting today in one of the back rooms."

Before I could even take in the meaning of her words, she disappeared from the room. A few minutes later she was back.

"I'll take you to see them," she said. "You can leave your suitcase with me."

I still hadn't absorbed her words as I followed her through a maze of halls before landing in front of a closed door. She opened it quietly, motioned for me to step inside and then left me there, standing in front of a half circle of a dozen men—whom I later learned were all revered leaders of the Methodist Church in the United Kingdom.

One of them motioned for me to take a seat in front of them. I did as I was directed, trying to get my head straight and think about what I could possibly say to them.

It was intimidating to be in the presence of all of these men. But I knew I wasn't there by accident. And if God had led me here, I figured He had a reason for doing so.

"How can we help you?" one of the men asked.

I took a deep breath to steady myself. "I've come to London to see how my life will go forward in the ministry," I said, forcing myself to look him directly in the eyes.

The man smiled and glanced at his colleagues.

"So why do want to pursue a life in the ministry?" another of the men questioned.

This was something I knew I could talk about. I started at the beginning, telling them of my life-changing conversion in my bedroom three years earlier, about my passion and devotion to my new-found faith, and about renting the hall in Killowen with my friends so we had a place to meet for prayer meetings, Bible study and worship.

I could tell my story resonated with the men because they listened intently and I noticed a few of them nodding as I spoke.

"Who sent you?" asked the man who had first addressed me. I learned later that I was talking with Arthur Ross, the Secretary of Candidates for the entire Methodist denomination.

"Nobody," I replied. "I've just come on my own.

"But I know Reverend Ludlow at the Methodist Church in Coleraine," I added quickly.

I watched him scribble something on a piece of paper.

"So where are you staying?" he asked.

I could hear my heart beating and feel the familiar rush of anxiety shooting through me. I didn't want to appear weak or have them feel sorry for me.

"Well I have no place to stay yet," I answered. "I'm looking for a job and I've got to do that. I was just passing by and saw the Methodist Central Hall that I've read about and thought I would come in here and have a look around. I didn't realize anyone was here but the lady at the desk was very kind to me, so now I'm sitting here and that's all I have to say."

For a few seconds, no one spoke. Then the men began chatting among themselves.

"Well let's call Ron Marshall at the Bermondsey mission and have him come get this young man and set him up with a place to stay," said Arthur Ross. "And let's get a call in to the Youth Department and get this young man a job to report to in the morning."

I was so stunned by their generosity and kindness that for a minute I couldn't speak. These men, who in normal circumstances would have been difficult to even get a meeting with, had taken it upon themselves to find me both a job and a place to live.

A few minutes later I was picked up by Ron Marshall's assistant and taken to a dormitory at the east end of the city where university students lived. It was a large dorm with partitions that separated one small room from the next. After getting me situated, the assistant gave me directions to the Methodist Church youth department in Ludgate Circus, one of the poorest neighborhoods in the city, and told me I would be starting the following morning.

I lay in bed that night listening to the bustle of students in the dorm and marveling at my good fortune. Then I closed my eyes and whispered a thank you prayer to God. I had put my trust in the Lord and taken a leap of faith by getting myself to London. He had taken care of the rest.

$\wp$

All you have to do is pick up that phone, dial that number and tell her who you are. That's all you have to do.

I repeated the words in my mind as I stared at the pay phone, trying to fight back the paralyzing anxiety shooting through me and force myself to dial the telephone number I'd found in the thick London phone directory.

This was the moment I'd been preparing myself for since learning that my birth mother was alive. It was the moment I'd fantasized about even when I thought she had been killed in the Blitz. So why was I wasting one more second?

My hands were shaking as I picked up the receiver, shoved the coins into the slot and slowly willed my fingers to turn the dialing wheel.

I heard the phone ring. Then I heard her voice.

"Hello," she said. It was a soft, sophisticated voice that carried traces of a Londonderry accent.

"I'm Raymond," I blurted into the receiver. "You left me with the Ross family when I was a baby and we were told you were killed in the Blitz. But I recently learned you were alive. I'm in London now and I would like to come see you."

There was a long pause and I could hear her thinking on the other end of the line. But her brother, Harry, must have called her and given her a heads up about me because when she spoke again, she didn't sound surprised.

"Look, I've got to work out the timing and right now doesn't work," she said. "But I can see you at 7 p.m. Sunday night."

I had waited through my first week of work before contacting her because I wanted to be settled. Now I had the entire weekend to wait before I would finally meet my mother.

I spent hours walking through my new neighborhood, thinking and rethinking about our meeting and the conversation we would have. *Would we feel an instant bond when we saw each other? Would we shake hands or would she try to hug me? And if she did, would I let her or would I hold back?*

Once our initial introduction was finished, I imagined that my mother would start by telling me how much she had missed me and how sorry she was for leaving me and not communicating with me. I wasn't sure what her answer would be when I asked her why she left me, but I was sure she had a good reason. And even if she didn't, I was ready to forgive her. That was in the past and we would move on from here.

My birth mother lived in Stoke Newington, a neighborhood on the other side of London about an hour bike ride from Bermondsey.

At 6 p.m., I climbed onto the bike I had borrowed from a student in the dormitory and started the cross-city trek I had mapped out earlier in the day.

Traffic clogged the bustling city streets and I concentrated on keeping the bike upright and away from the cars as I navigated my way through traffic. I crossed London Bridge and made my way through several neighborhoods before arriving at her address just before 7 p.m.

I climbed off the bike and stared at the apartment building in front of me; the building that contained my mother.

I heard myself inhale.

All you have to do is ring the doorbell, Raymond. That's all you have to do.

I once again played out our meeting in my mind. She would

answer the door, smile warmly at me and invite me in. We'd get through the awkwardness and then work on building a relationship.

I parked the bike in a nearby bike rack, forced myself to move toward the door and rang the bell to her apartment. Minutes later the door opened and I saw her: the woman I had memorized from that picture when I was a baby.

She didn't smile when she saw me. She didn't try to hug me. She didn't even reach out to shake my hand. There was no warmth in her eyes, no recognition that I was her son.

"Come in," she said in a formal tone.

My heart sunk so low in my gut it felt like I was lugging a large rock as I followed her through the hallway, up a flight of stairs and into her apartment. I clenched my hands into fists to keep them from trembling. I considered turning and running but I waited too long and had come too far for that.

The voice in my head began making excuses for her. *Maybe she's just nervous. Maybe she just needs a few minutes to adjust.*

I stepped into a small but nicely furnished apartment and took a seat at her kitchen table as directed.

"I'll put on some tea," she said, turning her back to me. "Are you hungry?"

I stared at my birth mother's back, biting the inside of my lip to keep from screaming. My mother was four feet away from me, but the distance between us was so great she might as well have been on the moon.

She asked me how I liked living in London and a few other meaningless questions while keeping her back toward me. Then she turned around, placed the tea and Welsh rarebit—melted cheese toast—in front of me and took a seat across the table.

"I left you with your father," she said, her tone measured and flat.

I stared at her, absorbing her words and waiting for her to continue. But that was it—her only explanation about my birth and her disappearance. She didn't say why; she didn't say she was sorry; she didn't say she missed me. It was clear from her body language that she viewed me as an unavoidable problem that she wanted to address and get over with as soon as possible.

When she spoke again, her voice was calm and dispassionate.

"I'm married now," she said. "And it would be better if you never came to see me again."

The rock that had been my heart was now a boulder of glass that had just shattered into a thousand jagged pieces. I could feel the glass cutting into me, carving away at my insides.

Stand up. Go. Get out of here, the voice screamed in my head. *SHE DOESN'T WANT YOU.*

"Okay," I heard myself say as I pushed myself out of the chair and moved toward the door. "Thank you for the tea."

Somehow I made it down the steps, out the door and onto the bike. I managed to navigate my way out of Stoke Newington, through the streets, back across London Bridge, and back to my dorm. I remember returning the bike to the student I had borrowed it from, heading to my partitioned room and collapsing on the bed.

I was paralyzed with pain. It wasn't just my heart that had shattered. It was as though she had ripped out my soul.

My mind raced through the five years since I had learned of her existence: the countless hours I had spent thinking about her and fantasizing about the friendship and life we could have together. I thought about the lengths I had gone to uncover the truth—that she was alive and well, living in London—and about how I had left everything I knew behind and made the move to London so that I could finally meet her. I had been so fixated on reuniting with her that it never occurred to me that she had purposely discarded me from her life and wanted nothing to do with me. I may have been her blood son, but to her I was no more than a stranger who could be avoided and forgotten about.

My head was on fire. The pain and humiliation was too much to process. I had to make it go away.

The only saving thought was that I hadn't told anyone about my quest to find my birth mother. I could just erase this incident from my mind, pretend it never happened and go back to the story I had always been told.

My birth mother loved me and wanted me but she was dead. She was killed in the London blitz. She died before she could come back for me.

My faith kept me going on the days when the depression and pain felt too heavy to bear, and I found solace in prayer and hymns.

A couple of weeks after starting my job in the books section at the Methodist Youth Department, Arthur Ross summoned me back to Methodist Central Hall.

"Why didn't you tell us you were a Lay Preacher on Trial?" he asked.

His words caught me by surprise and my mind went into overdrive. What did he mean Lay Preacher on Trial? I thought about the little church I had started with my friends. Was that what he was talking about?

"I don't know," I replied finally, trying to sound nonchalant. "I guess I didn't think it was important."

"Of course it's important," he said. "It means we've got to get you busy preaching."

He explained that he had written to Reverend Ludlow in Coleraine to inquire about me and that it was the Reverend who had told him about my Lay Preacher on Trial status.

The only preaching I had done for Reverend Ludlow was leading the children's story that one Sunday morning. But thanks to his recommendation and kind words about me, I began receiving invitations to speak in Methodist churches throughout London. My life was suddenly so full that I didn't have time to dwell on my birth mother's rejection. When I wasn't delivering books to other publishers and bookstores throughout the city, giving sermons or teaching Sunday School classes, I spent my time exploring the city and hanging out with friends I'd made at the dorm and through the Methodist youth department.

But as the months passed, I felt nagging doubts building inside me. The people I had encountered in the Methodist Church were the kindest people I had ever met. They had taken me in as a stranger, set me up with a job and a place to live, and had given me the opportunity to flourish and grow in their ministry. Instead of just preaching the principles of the gospel, they devoted their lives to helping people in need. Many of them were actively involved in the Labor Movement and dedicated themselves to helping the poor, homeless and disenfranchised. Unlike some of the staunch conservative churches in Coleraine, Methodists were allowed to attend films and they were less judgmental overall.

I admired their focus on helping people in need and vowed to follow their example in my own ministry. But from a faith standpoint, there was one key issue I couldn't reconcile. Some of the Methodists I encountered didn't believe in the Virgin Birth. The story of the Virgin Birth had always been at the foundation of my faith and now I was beginning to question their beliefs.

I headed back to Coleraine for the Christmas holidays and re-united with Jackie, Billy and the rest of my friends. They were still running our small church in Killowen and slowly building a congregation. It felt good to be back with them and by the time I returned to London after the holidays, I knew what I had to do.

As much as I loved the Methodist leaders I had met, pursuing a ministry in the Methodist church wasn't my calling. In early February I packed up my suitcase, said goodbye and headed back to Coleraine.

I quickly picked up where I had left off—helping my friends to expand the congregation at our small church in Killowen and continuing my open air preaching near the coast. I also began speaking regularly in congregations throughout Northern Ireland. I knew more than ever that my future was in the ministry and realized I needed formal training. But when I began researching Bible colleges in the United States, the financial hurdles were so great I didn't know how I could possibly get there.

It was Dr. John Wesley White, a well-known evangelist who I had become friendly with, who came up with the answer for me.

"You should think about attending the Full Gospel Bible Institute in Eston, Saskatchewan in Canada," he said when I told him about my desire to attend Bible college. "I know the principal there and could write to him on your behalf."

As soon as I heard the word Canada I felt a rush of energy. When I was in grade school, one of the pictures that covered the walls was of the Fraser River cutting through the city of Vancouver in Western Canada. I had been so taken by its beauty that I vowed to see it in person one day.

My thoughts jumped to David Livingstone and his life as a missionary explorer. I craved adventure and wanted to get out and see the world. And now the opportunity was presenting itself.

Beyond Dr. White's connections at the Bible college, Canada was in need of immigrants and had established a program that made it easier for people to come to the country. For only ten pounds down, I could board a ship that would take me from Ireland to Canada and had up to two years to finish paying off the two hundred pound fare.

In the summer of 1955, three years after boarding the vessel from Belfast to my new life in England, I once again found myself on a ship—this time headed for Canada. It was a six-day voyage that would take me across the Atlantic Ocean and deliver me to Montreal, where I would catch a train that would eventually take me to my new life in the Saskatchewan.

Once again I had only a few pounds to my name and no idea how I was going to provide for myself or earn enough money to attend the Bible college. I also had no idea how I would come up with the money to pay for my cross-Atlantic journey.

But as I walked the deck of the ship and looked out at the waves that would carry me to the next phase of my life, I felt calm and confident. What I now knew for certain was that the scripture I had read all those years ago was true: *All things are possible to him who believe.*

All I had to do was pray to God for guidance and then take that leap of faith by taking that first step. The rest was up to Him. And I knew He would get me where I needed to go.

Above: Ray's foster parents, Lavina and Jimmy Ross. Right: Ray's paternal grandfather outside his barber shop in Killowen. Below: Ray standing by the Killowen mailbox where he played postman as a child.

Above: Ray in front of Culmore Castle, where he went to search for his biological mother.

Above: Guildhall in Londonderry, where Ray fainted while trying to share his testimony.

Above left: Ray as a teenager. **Above right:** Ray's biological mother, Margaret Barnett. **Below:** Ray in front of the church he attended as a child in Killowen.

Above: Ray pictured with Jackie and Billy Dinsmore. **Below:** Ray's friends and co-founders of their youth church.

My Ministry

...

5

Fall 1966

I HAD EXPECTED KRISTA TO tell me about her trip behind the Iron Curtain to visit her grandmother. Instead, she dropped a bombshell.

"Are you aware of the situation those Soviet Christians are in?" she asked. "It's horrible, Ray. Many I talked with have been beaten and harassed and some have even been imprisoned. They have absolutely nothing. They've given up everything for their faith."

Krista, a pretty Canadian journalist in her early twenties, had traveled to Sweden to cover the Christian Businessmen's Airlift Convention I'd helped organize on the heels of a similar event I'd orchestrated in London the year before. Like the London Airlift, hundreds of Christian businessmen and pastors of various denominations had flown into Stockholm to share the charismatic renewal taking hold throughout Christianity. As part of the mass outreach effort, we had sent teams into communities throughout Scandinavia. We'd also managed to secure an inroad into the Eastern Bloc country of Estonia and Krista had asked if she could accompany the team.

Securing the visa necessary to get her into the country had been a difficult feat because Krista hadn't originally disclosed to me that her real reason for wanting to go to Estonia was because she had a grandmother there that she had never met. But that story came out when the Soviets denied her entry. Though she was an atheist, we had prayed together and I had advised her to go back and tell them the truth. Miraculously, the Soviets had issued her the visa the second time around and I had assumed that she would spend all of her time in Estonia getting to know her grandmother.

Instead, Krista told me she had accompanied the team to a meeting at one of the registered Christian churches, where the pastor's son and daughter had handpicked her to attend an underground church deep in the forest.

It was there, away from the prying eyes and ears of the authorities, that she had learned of the relentless persecution and suffering Soviet Christians were being forced to endure.

Krista told me she was approached by one Christian after another, who recounted harrowing stories of harassment, deprivation and beatings by KGB agents. She said they also told her about friends and loved ones who had been arrested and were being starved and tortured in Siberian gulags for their faith.

Before leaving, Krista said the pastor's children had pulled her aside and asked if she would carry out letters documenting their plight in hopes of finding someone in the West who could help them.

"It's unbelievable," Krista said, wrapping up her story. "They risked a great deal bringing me to that underground church. The people wept at the sight of someone from the free world. It meant everything to them just to know that somebody cared."

She reached into her bag, pulled out the stack of letters she had been entrusted with and pushed them into my hand.

"Ray, these people are in desperate need of help," she said. "Why don't you help them?"

The irony that Krista—the one non-believer in our group—had been singled out as the person the Soviet Christians trusted to help them share their struggles and letters with the world in hopes of getting help was not lost on me. I knew God helped her get into the country for that reason and I spent the ten-hour flight back to Canada replaying her words in my mind. My thoughts bounced from images of the suffering Soviet Christians, who were willing to risk their lives and freedom to practice their faith, to my current ministry and purpose.

In the eleven years since I had boarded that ship to Canada to attend Bible college, my life had followed a trajectory that combined my love for preaching with travel ministry. After a rocky start that had included a year off to serve as a fill-in minister at a rural Canadian church and a temporary move back to Coleraine, I had finally graduated. Along the way I had met Ruth, gotten married and now had two small children: Robert and Rheanne. Our life was a cobbled together existence that consisted of numerous guest speaking engagements at churches throughout Canada, the US and the United Kingdom, and a day job at a local travel agency in Alberta—where we had settled—in which I led faith-based tours to the holy land and other parts of the world.

It was during a 1962 trip to the World's Fair in Seattle that I was introduced to the Full Gospel Businessmen, which led me to start a local chapter. That, in turn, had inspired me to organize the Airlift to London.

Life felt good enough. I was becoming a known name in evangelical circles and the invitations to speak at larger churches and venues were growing. But I had been reluctant to help organize the Stockholm event and had spent most of the convention feeling empty and lost. Like the London Airlift, the Stockholm convention had been a huge success. But the logistics and administrative work involved magnified my weaknesses. I wasn't organized, couldn't write reports and was constantly putting out fires that resulted from my lack of organizational skills. Beyond that, I was beginning to question whether the work I was doing was relevant. I often thought back to my days with the Methodists and their focus on helping the needy and disenfranchised.

The convention was winding down by the time the team headed into Estonia and I had spent hours in my hotel room in prayer, asking God for guidance on how to proceed with my ministry.

Now, here was Krista, presenting me with the answer I had been searching for. I knew without question that God had used her as a messenger and that He was directing me to help the Soviet Christians. The only question I had as I flipped through the stack of letters written in a language I assumed was Russian, was how?

Back in Canada, I continued to accept speaking engagements and continued my work in the travel industry while searching for someone who could help me translate the documents. After an extensive search, I found an African university student who was fluent in Russian and willing to translate the letters for five cents a word.

I was so short on money that it took months for me to scrape together enough to get all of the letters translated. But when they were done, I had a stack of compelling documents that detailed the atrocities being committed against Soviet Christians. The documents also listed the names and arrest dates of everyone who had been imprisoned because of their public display of faith.

Each letter opened the same way: *Dear friends in the West*. I had been praying for the Soviet Christians since the Stockholm convention and had continued to ask God for guidance on how I could help. Now, as I stared at those words, an idea began forming in my mind:

I would start a human rights organization that focused on helping persecuted and imprisoned Christians behind the Iron Curtain. And I would call it Friends in the West.

My idea for the ministry was simple. I would start a prayer campaign on behalf of the imprisoned and suffering Christians and get tens of thousands of Christians in the West to pray for them. Along with providing hope and comfort for the Soviet Christians, I saw the prayer campaign as a way to generate such widespread awareness and outrage over their plight that the world community would feel compelled to step in to help.

Ruth and I began the long, arduous process of filing for a non-profit organization. We had recently moved to Vancouver, and our kitchen table became the organization headquarters. Along with officially establishing Friends in the West, we began writing hundreds of letters to pastors we knew, explaining our mission and asking for help in the form of donations and prayers. I also began lining up speaking engagements at any church that would have me in hopes of spreading the word.

I knew that if I really wanted to make a difference, I needed to travel into the Eastern Bloc countries and meet personally with the Christian community. I needed to capture their stories, establish contacts for ongoing communication, and provide them with hope by letting them know that Christians in the free world were praying for them and working on their behalf.

I began taking three-week road trips throughout the United States, utilizing a special airline promotion available to non-US residents. For $150, I could fly standby on small regional airplanes to anywhere in the continental United States during that twenty-one day period.

At first, people were confused by what I was trying to do.

"Prayer is the point," I would say when they asked me what I hoped to accomplish with the prayer campaign. "Through the power of prayer, we will eventually stop the persecution and get the imprisoned Christians released."

It took time, but by the spring of 1972, Friends in the West was an official organization and congregations in churches throughout the US, Canada and the UK were praying regularly on behalf of the suffering Christians living behind the Iron Curtain. I had also managed to scrape together enough funding for my first trip into an Eastern Bloc country, and was headed to Prague to meet with persecuted Christians and see what I could do to help an imprisoned pastor in the Czech Republic.

I boarded the plane in London and was about an hour into my journey when a flight attendant stopped by my seat and asked if I would like coffee. As she handed me the steaming cup, her bracelet caught my eye. It was a heavy, silver-toned bracelet and appeared to have something inscribed on it.

"Can you tell me about your bracelet?" I asked her. "It's unusual, isn't it?"

The flight attendant smiled.

"Yes," she replied, moving her wrist closer to me so I could examine it. "It's a POW bracelet. The man whose name is inscribed on it is in a Vietnamese prison camp. The idea is to wear it until he's released."

I studied the inscribed name and felt excitement rushing through me. This was exactly what I needed for Friends in the West—prayer bracelets inscribed with the names of the imprisoned Christians.

A verse from a scripture (Hebrews 13:3 NLT) that had been the basis for Friends in the West popped into my mind: *Remember those in prison, as if you were there yourself. Remember also those being mistreated, as if you felt their pain in your own bodies.*

What better way to remember and feel for those being mistreated and imprisoned than to wear a bracelet bearing his or her name?

I didn't know where to get the bracelets made or how much it was going to cost. But I knew for certain that this was the next step. I spent the next two days in Prague, meeting with Christians, telling them about the thousands of prayers being offered on their behalf and finding out all I could about the imprisoned pastor. Then I boarded the plane back to London, where I immediately placed a call to my friend Jerry Jensen, who had been volunteering his time to help me.

"We need to figure out who can manufacture these bracelets for us," I said, after telling him about the POW bracelet I'd seen on the flight. "I'm not sure where we'll get the money for it. But we'll find a way."

After numerous phone calls, we were able to track down Accurate Dial, a manufacturer in Glendale, California, that could handle the job. Within weeks, our first batch of bracelets arrived—all inscribed with strange-sounding names such as Rodoslavov, Rytikov and Kriukchov. Unlike the heavy POW bracelets, we worked with the manufacturer to find an affordable, bendable silver aluminum metal that was shipped flat in two bracelet sizes: large and small. Ruth, the kids and I then bent the metal into curved bracelets using a small forming device the manufacturer had sent us, and I began offering them up for donations at churches were I spoke. The bracelets were an immediate hit. Soon thousands of Christians throughout the United States, Canada and the UK were wearing them. We also began writing petitions on behalf of the Soviet Christians and got word to our underground contacts of the prayer campaign and efforts underway.

I was frustrated that they were still suffering, still being persecuted for their faith. But if nothing else, I knew our prayer campaign was providing the Soviet Christians with something many of them had lost: hope.

I was exhausted and discouraged by the time I arrived in Nashville to speak at the Grand Ole Opry House in the summer of 1975.

I should have been elated. It was a huge venue and my message to encourage prayer for Soviet Christians was being broadcast live over the Grand Ole Opry radio network, enabling me to reach thousands of believers and numerous connected Christians in the country music world.

But I had been living on the road for months—going from church to church to share the plight of the Soviet Christians and plead for prayer and donations—and it had worn me down. Ruth and I now had our third child, Rhonda, but I was gone so much that I rarely got to spend time with my family. On top of that, money was so tight that it was a struggle to pay our house payment and utility bills. And while the prayer campaign and bracelets had taken hold, progress seemed so slow that I felt like all I was doing was making chicken scratches.

In the three years since officially launching Friends in the West, I had managed to secure a small office and was getting inundated with letters smuggled out of the Soviet Union from Christians detailing suffocating oppression, brutal beatings and violent arrests. Their letters always ended with pleas for help and their continued suffering was eating away at me. Though a few imprisoned Christians had been released since the start of the prayer campaign, more were being imprisoned and the persecution seemed to be intensifying.

One case in particular kept hammering away in my mind. It was that of Georgi Vins, a well-known Baptist pastor from Kiev who had been leading the underground church movement there. Vins, who was in his late forties, had already served a three-year prison term and had recently been arrested again and sentenced to five years in a hard labor camp, followed by an additional five years in internal exile.

I didn't know what I could do to get him released. But I had heard from my underground contacts that his health had already deteriorated in the few months he had been in the labor camp and I wasn't sure how much longer he could withstand the harsh slave conditions.

I shared Georgi Vins' story and desperate plight with the crowd that packed the historic Nashville venue and then followed it up with my usual plea for prayers and donations.

As I was speaking the words—trying to inspire action despite my discouragement—my thoughts suddenly locked on the recent televised Watergate hearings. I had been impressed with one of the attorneys and remembered hearing that he was from Nashville.

As soon as the service was over, I tracked down the local pastor and asked if he could connect me with the attorney, James Foster Neal, so I could get his advice.

"Sure," the pastor replied. "I'll call you with his details later this evening."

I went to sleep that night still exhausted, discouraged and beaten down. But the next morning I pulled myself together as I always did and made a call to the attorney—who agreed to meet with me in his office.

He didn't have any magic solutions that would put an end to the suffering and get Georgi Vins released. But he did have an idea for me.

"I would start with the US mission to the United Nations and go from there," he suggested.

This wasn't the first time the United Nations had come up. The letters that flooded my small office often addressed their pleas for help to the international government organization.

As tired as I was, I knew what I had to do next. I thanked the attorney for his time, packed up my bags and headed to the airport for a standby flight to New York. As soon as I landed, I made my way to the United Nations headquarters.

It took several inquiries and hours of waiting, but I eventually found myself in the office of Guy A. Wiggins, who headed the US Human Rights Mission to the United Nations.

Guy was a tall, distinguished-looking man in his mid-fifties who was clearly well educated. He was also personable and down-to-earth and we hit it off instantly.

Guy listened intently as I laid out the situation facing Georgi Vins and other imprisoned Soviet Christians. But when I asked what he could do to help me, he shook his head and let out a cynical laugh.

"I can tell you one thing," he said. "If you think the United Nations is going to be of any use to you, forget it. This place is a dead end when it comes to human rights in the USSR. The Soviets are members of the UN security council and have veto power."

Though it wasn't what I wanted to hear, I appreciated his candor. We spent the next few minutes in easy conversation, sharing our background, vision and passions. Guy told me he had been with the State Department for eighteen years and was deeply concerned about human rights. But he also told me about his love of painting. He explained that his father was a highly regarded American impressionist painter and said that he had always been torn between public service and art. He said it was this constant pull toward painting that had recently brought him to the decision to soon retire from his government post so he could pursue his passion.

Eventually our conversation returned to Georgi Vins and the plight of all Soviet Christians.

"If you want my opinion," Guy said, "you need to work through the United States legislative process."

I laughed, thinking about how unlikely it was that I had managed to find my way to the United Nations and wondering how I would possibly navigate Capitol Hill.

"I can appreciate what you're saying, but I'm not exactly an expert in the United States political system," I said finally. "Too bad you already have a job."

Guy didn't say anything for a minute. But I could see him thinking.

"I'll tell you what, Ray. Why don't we talk about this again after I've had some time to think about it? I have an idea we could get a lot accomplished if we worked together."

An immediate alliance was formed. Over the next few months, Guy began making phone calls and inquiries to contacts in Congress while I pulled together as many official documents and letters I could find that detailed the atrocities being committed against Soviet Christians.

A few months later, the two of us were on Capitol Hill, sitting in the office of John Buchanan, a Congressman from Alabama who had once served as a Baptist minister. Congressman Buchanan was a Republican with a charismatic personality and a passion for human rights issues. He worked across the aisle on various civil rights initiatives—such as teaming with Democratic Congressman Charles Weltner to spearhead an investigation of the Klu Klux Klan. He was also concerned with global issues and served on the House Foreign

Affairs Committee.

The Congressman listened with interest as we talked about the relentless persecution Soviet Christians faced and our hope that we could get the US government to put pressure on the Soviet Union to end the harassment and release Georgi Vins and other religious prisoners. When we were through talking, I presented him with the stack of documents I had gathered.

Congressman Buchanan spent a few minutes combing through them and reading bits and pieces of the reports. But when he finally spoke, he didn't sound hopeful.

"If you write something up, I can get it entered into the Congressional Record," he said. "But that's about the extent of what I can do."

I tried not to let his words deflate me. But it had taken a lot of time and effort to get to this point and I couldn't see what good it would do to write something down on paper and have it entered into the Congressional Record. But since we had come this far, I figured it couldn't hurt.

Guy and I thanked Congressman Buchanan for his time and went for a cup of coffee, where we spent the next hour scribbling down verbiage for a resolution on the back of a paper bag. Our message was simple. It said that the United States Congress condemned what the USSR was doing to Pastor Georgi Vins, his family and other Christians who were being persecuted and imprisoned for their faith. It called on Soviet officials to release Georgi Vins and stop the religious persecution.

Once we were finished, we left the paper bag with the Congressman's secretary and headed home, hopeful that something would come of our efforts.

∽

I was in my Vancouver office a few weeks later when the call came.

"Ray, what on earth have you been doing?" Congressman Buchanan's voice thundered through the receiver. "It's unbelievable. I introduced your Resolution and there are more than a hundred Congressmen from both parties who want to co-sponsor the bill."

I could feel his excitement over the phone line. I wasn't sure what it meant to have so many members of Congress interested in the resolution, but I could tell by Congressman Buchanan's reaction that it was a big deal.

"Well, I'm praying and getting other people to pray," I replied.

The Congressman laughed. "Well, you are clearly doing something right because we want to hold Foreign Affairs Committee hearings on this. Can you find us some pastors who have recently been expelled from the Soviet Union who could testify at the hearings?"

I wasn't sure what this latest development meant for the Soviet Christians, but I sensed something powerful was underway. I hung up the phone and immediately went to work.

The hearings were scheduled for June 24th and 30th, which gave me three months to locate pastors who had recently been expelled from the USSR and could come to Washington to testify at the Congressional hearings. I wrote to a Norwegian contact for help and was soon put in contact with Yanis Smits and David Klassen, both Soviet Baptist pastors who had been exiled and were living in West Germany.

The men gladly agreed to testify and I booked their airline tickets to Washington, figuring I'd be able to come up with the money to pay for their tickets by the time the hearings arrived. But with only two days to go, I had not been able to scrape together the necessary funds. On top of it all, I was in the hospital, recovering from emergency surgery after a severe gall bladder attack.

I was trapped in a hospital bed with an IV dripping into my arm. The area around my incision was on fire and I was so weak I could barely shift my body. I was sweating, but I couldn't tell if it was from a fever or from the knowledge that Yanis Smits and David Klassen would be arriving at the Frankfort Airport in Germany within 36 hours, expecting to have airline tickets waiting for them.

I pushed the button for a nurse, who in turn tracked down my doctor.

"I need to get out of here," I told him, struggling to get into a sitting position. "I've got to be in Washington."

The doctor looked at me like I was crazy. But I knew I didn't have a choice.

Against his advice, I checked myself out of the hospital and drove myself across the border to Seattle to catch a regional standby flight to Phoenix. I knew a pastor there who I hoped could help. But his response was the same as everyone else I had approached.

"I'm sorry, Ray," he said. "I would love to help but we are so tight on money and have so many of our own needs that we don't have any to spare."

I was sweating so much from my weakened condition that it was hard to think. I just wanted to crawl into bed, close my eyes and escape the nightmare. But there was no time for rest.

I headed back to the airport, fighting the waves of despair that were crashing over me. I had only a few hours to come up with the airfare. What if I couldn't do it? I had made a commitment to both the pastors and Congressman Buchanan. What if I couldn't deliver?

My next standby flight routed me to Chicago, where I would catch another standby fight to Washington D.C. I spent most of the journey whispering pleading prayers and wracking my brain for a solution. I mentally flipped through the Rolodex of pastors I knew, trying to come up with a name I hadn't already contacted.

Just as my plane started its descent into Chicago, I remembered a conversation I'd had with a pastor in Seattle a year or so earlier. She had told me that if Friends in the West were ever in urgent need, she would find a way to help.

I didn't know why I hadn't thought of her before. I also didn't know if she would even remember that conversation. But my situation was definitely urgent and she was my last shot. I had less than an hour to catch my flight to Washington D.C. and by the time it landed, I would be too late. The flight from Frankfurt would already be en route.

I pushed my way off the plane and rushed to the first bank of payphones I could find.

I pumped in a handful of quarters and began dialing the number, silently praying that someone would answer the phone.

I heard myself exhale when Pat, the pastor's assistant, answered.

"Oh, good, I'm so glad someone is there," I said. "Could I speak with Pastor Baker please?"

"I'm sorry, she's not in right now," the woman replied. "But is there anything I can help you with?"

I took a deep breath, trying to calm myself so I wouldn't sound as desperate and panicked as I felt.

"Well it's a bit of an emergency," I said. "Would it be possible for you to help me with some airfare expenses?"

I quickly explained the circumstances to the assistant and then braced myself for her reaction. I wasn't even sure that she had the power to help me and I knew that the safe answer was "no."

I expected at least some hesitation and push back. But there was none.

"Don't worry, Ray," she said simply. "We'll take care of it."

The next afternoon I was at the D.C. airport with Congressman Buchanan's press secretary, picking up the two exiled pastors. And the following morning, we all headed to Capitol Hill for the Foreign Affairs Committee hearings.

I had expected the hearings to take place in a small conference room with a few key committee members. Instead, we were ushered into a large assembly hall packed with lawmakers, journalists and human rights activists from all corners of the country. Along with Yanis Smits and David Klassen, witnesses included several professors and a research director for a D.C.-based human rights organization.

I stood in the back of the room, transfixed by the riveting testimony. I could feel the solidarity of everyone who had crammed into that room on behalf of the Soviet Christians, and by the time the hearings were over, it was clear that the resolution was headed for a vote in Congress. This intention was made official on September 2, 1976, when the committee's report was formerly printed.

The resolution that Guy Wiggins and I had scribbled down on the back of that paper bag was passed by the House of Representatives on September 20, 1976, by a vote of 381 to 2.

Ten days later, as the last order of business before their Congressional break, the United States Senate passed the resolution by a unanimous vote. Two men particularly instrumental in getting the bill pushed through the Senate were Senators Hubert Humphrey, Minnesota, and Scoop Jackson, Washington State.

Gratitude swept through me as I absorbed the news. The most

powerful country in the world had taken a stand on behalf of Georgi Vins and the other Soviet Christians. The United States had stood up to the Soviet Union and had made it clear that continued religious persecution would not be tolerated.

I didn't know where the Resolution might lead. But I knew that it had been God's doing that had propelled the Resolution forward. And I trusted that He had a plan.

6

1975

I T WAS A PRAYER of desperation I had thrown up to heaven in hopes that God would hear me.

"Lord, if I'm on the right track, somehow let me know," I had pleaded. "Because I'm ready to call it quits."

I was in Northern Ireland on a two-day layover before heading to Yugoslavia to meet with yet another group of persecuted Christians. But I was so discouraged and exhausted I was on the verge of giving up.

After years of struggling to support my family on the five and ten dollar donations that sporadically arrived in the mail while fighting to keep Friends in the West afloat, I had finally reached my breaking point. I was fed up with not having two pennies to rub together, with constantly having to worry about how to pay our mortgage and buy groceries. I was tired of sleeping on airport benches and cleaning up in airport washrooms because I couldn't afford a motel room. And I was sick of fighting so hard to help the Soviet Christians and having so little to show for it.

It was early 1975—a year and a half before the Congressional resolution was passed—and nothing I had done to date had seemed to make a bit of difference for Christians living behind the Iron Curtain. Despite the thousands of prayer bracelets being worn on their behalf, the endless prayers being offered daily and the public awareness about their plight that I had managed to generate through the media, they continued to be harassed, imprisoned and tortured for their faith.

I had borrowed a friend's van for the day, hoping that a drive to the coast would somehow lift my spirits and help me find clarity. Now, just minutes after begging God for some sort of a signal, something inside me was urging me to head to Culmore Point to visit the old castle where my biological mother had lived.

My friend, Bobby Hill, who had accompanied me to the coast, agreed to make the trek with me. But as we waited in snarled lines to pass through the heavily guarded military checkpoints that clogged the city of Londonderry, I could feel my depression deepen and I wondered what had gotten into me.

The guerrilla war raging throughout Northern Ireland made travel a virtual impossibility, especially in cities such as Londonderry that were close to the border of the Republic of Ireland.

Rain pounded on the windshield, adding to the gloom of the standstill traffic and the grim-looking soldiers with their automatic rifles. But I couldn't make myself turn around.

It took more than three hours to travel the thirty-five-mile journey to Culmore Point and when we finally arrived, it was nearly dusk.

The fog was so dense near the banks of the River Foyle that I had a hard time making out the road in front of me. I parked as close as I could get to the old stone tower, which was now boarded up and clearly vacant. My gut tightened as I thought about the one other time I had visited this place.

Once again I asked myself why I had suffered through hours of

ln't sound as de-
ght as well take a

ve headed to the
, trying to get a
arded windows.
e building when
man—emerging

and was dressed
in Southwester rain gear. He looked exactly like the old fisherman
featured on the cough candy tins I sometimes purchased.

Given the constant IRA bombings in the area, I knew it didn't
bode well to have strangers lurking around a remote, abandoned
building. I headed toward the old man, waving as I walked so he
would realize I meant no harm.

"Good evening," I said, forcing a smile on my face. "I'm Ray
Barnett. I'm just here looking at this old castle."

The old man looked me over and then nodded his acknowledg-
ment.

"Yes," he said, motioning toward the structure. "It's a historical
building. It belongs to the Irish Society but they aren't doing a good
job of taking care of it."

I exhaled, relieved that he didn't have a problem with me being
there.

"Yes, I can see that," I replied. "I'm just here because my mother, Margaret, lived here and I wanted to check it out."

The old fisherman looked at me like he was expecting me.

"Yes, that's right," he said.

His words caught me off guard. *He knew my mother?* I hadn't spoken her name in years—hadn't allowed myself to think of her at all. The pain from her rejection nearly twenty-five years earlier had cut so deep that I had buried the entire incident of our London encounter deep inside me and had half convinced myself that it had never happened. Over the years, whenever the subject of my birth mother came up, I repeated the story I had been told by the Rosses: that my mother had died in the London blitz.

It was the story I repeated now to the fisherman, explaining that I was still a baby when she was killed.

The old man looked at me like I was crazy.

"She's not dead," he said. "She's living in New Rochelle, New York."

His words slammed into me, but they were nothing compared to the massive tidal wave that followed.

"You have a sister, too," he said.

I stared at the old fisherman, too shocked to respond. Then his words began seeping in and I could feel my heart bouncing inside me.

The old man continued to talk; so full of information it was as though he had my family tree laid out in front of him. He told me that my Uncle Harry, who I had met as a teenager, was also living in New York, and said that I had an aunt who now lived in New Zealand.

"I've got their postal addresses if you want them," he added.

It was so mind-boggling I was having a hard time comprehending what was happening. I rummaged through my pocket for a piece of paper. All I could find were a couple of green 4x4 flyers advertising the prayer bracelets. I grabbed one, found a pen, and started scribbling on the back of the flyer as fast as I could write while the old fisherman rattled off the addresses from memory.

By the time he was done, I had a treasure trove of information on my biological family and their whereabouts. But the piece I wanted most was missing.

"So do you know where my sister is?" I asked, unconsciously holding my breath.

The fisherman shook his head.

"I'm sorry," he said. "She was adopted by a couple when she was a little girl.

"But I know the man's last name was Wells and that he worked for the Tulbury Dredging Company," he added. "And I know your sister's name was Iris, but I think they changed it to Kathleen."

The crushing despair that had been bearing down on me was gone. I was floating on such a high that the enormity of what had just transpired didn't fully hit me until we were back on the road, once again waiting in snarled traffic lines to get through a military checkpoint.

I had asked God to somehow show me that I was on the right track and had been delivered the biggest miracle of my life. I had a SISTER.

I headed to Yugoslavia as planned, no longer doubting that I was on the right path with my ministry. As soon as I was back in Northern Ireland, I began my quest to find my sister.

I started by combing through a London phone directory, searching for Tulbury Dredging. The name didn't exist but after combing through all of the names starting with a letter "T" for a second time, I came across a company named "Tilbury Engineering."

It was the closest name I could find and I figured it was worth a shot. I dialed the number to the engineering firm and asked the lady who answered if the company had ever been involved in dredging.

"Oh yes," she replied. "In fact we used to be called Tilbury Contracting and Dredging."

I could feel the smile breaking open across my face. I knew I was on to something.

"I don't know if you keep records from before the war," I continued, "but I'm looking for someone I think worked for you. His last name was Wells. Is there a way to look up the name?"

The woman chuckled.

"Oh I don't have to look that up," she replied. "He was the chief engineer of this firm, but he just died. The board members are just back from his funeral at this moment."

I couldn't believe what I was hearing. The man who adopted my sister forty years earlier had been the firm's chief engineer? I knew this was God's answer to my prayers, guiding me toward the information I needed to find.

My heart was pounding and I could feel elation sweeping through me. I told the woman the first thing I could think of that would get her to unlock the next clue.

"My name is Ray Barnett," I said. "I'm a clergyman and I'm just trying to trace my roots. I think the Wells have information that could help me. Would you be able to put me in touch with Mr. Wells' family?"

I could hear the woman thinking.

"Well," she said, "I know he has a wife and daughter. I'll call Mrs. Wells and see if it's okay to give you her details."

Within a few days, I had the phone number for the woman who had the ability to reunite me with my sister. When I arrived in London the next week, I called Mrs. Wells and repeated the explanation I had given to the secretary at the Engineering firm. I told her I thought she could help me in my quest and asked if I could drop by for a visit.

"That would be fine," she replied in a proper British accent.

"You can come by tomorrow afternoon."

Mrs. Wells lived in Sutton Surrey, a posh neighborhood in the suburbs of London. I was staying with my journalist friend, Dan Wooding, and he offered to drive me there and be with me for moral support.

The house was a beautiful two-story brick home that sat on an expansive, perfectly manicured lawn and garden.

I stared at the large brick structure in front of me, trying to formulate the words I would say. Behind those brick walls was my sister's adopted mother. I knew I was catching her by surprise and that it wasn't going to be an easy conversation. But I also knew God had guided me here for a reason.

I whispered a prayer in my mind and then reached for the passenger door.

"Pray for me," I said to Dan as I stepped out of the car.

I headed to the house and knocked on the door. An older, elegant-looking woman answered.

"Oh, my sister is having a pre-birthday cocktail party in the garden," she said when I introduced myself and explained why I was there.

I was shown to a drawing room to wait while she stepped outside to talk with her sister. A few minutes later, Mrs. Wells entered the room.

"How can I help you?" she asked.

I looked at Mrs. Wells, trying to determine where to start. She was an elderly woman—probably close to eighty—and I knew she had just suffered through the death of her husband. I didn't want to upset her. But I had to find my sister.

I decided to get right to the point.

"Through a series of circumstances, I've discovered that I have a sister," I said, locking my eyes on hers. "According to information I have, you and your husband adopted her."

I watched Mrs. Wells stiffen in her seat.

"Oh no," she said. "We have a daughter but she wasn't adopted."

The polite smile had disappeared from her face and I could see the worry and fear in her eyes. It hurt me to know I was causing her pain. But I had to keep going.

"Look Mrs. Wells, I know this is hard for you and I won't do anything to disturb you," I said. "I'm just trying to find out the truth. I know that my sister's birth name was Iris and I was told you changed it to Kathleen."

"That's not right," she blurted indignantly. "We changed it to Catherine."

We sat in silence for what felt like hours. I knew she would have done anything to take her words back.

"Well," Mrs. Wells said finally, "I couldn't tell you where she is because she suffers from severe migraine headaches and this would just make it worse."

I let this information sink into my mind and then once again locked my eyes on Mrs. Wells.

"Do you think it's a possibility that she suffers the migraines because she has more memories than you know and wonders who she is?" I prodded quietly.

Mrs. Wells glared at me defiantly and I knew our conversation and visit was over.

"It's okay," I said as I stood up to leave. "I realize this is very painful for you and as I mentioned before, I won't do anything to disturb you. But I know that God has guided me to this point and wants me to find my sister. And someday I am going to meet her, however God makes it happen."

I was back in London nearly two years later when the next clue finally came. It was delivered through a phone call from Dan, who was so excited he was nearly shouting into the receiver.

"You're not going to believe this," he said. "I was just telling one of our columnists about you and your search to find your sister and it turns out that your sister is her COUSIN and Mrs. Wells is her aunt. She was completely taken by surprise. She said no one in her family knew that Catherine was adopted. She's going home tonight to talk with her husband to decide what she should do."

I was swimming in so many emotions it was hard to separate them. I had spent every day since that encounter with Mrs. Wells thinking about Catherine. I wondered what she looked like; what she was passionate about; what her life had been like growing up. I wondered what memories she had of our mother and what, if anything, she knew about me. Most of all, I wondered how she would react when I finally found her. Would she be excited? Or, like my mother, would she view me as an unwanted secret from the past?

When the columnist returned to work the next day, she told Dan that out of loyalty to her aunt, she realized she couldn't give us Catherine's contact information. But then she dropped a hint. She told Dan that Catherine's married name was France and said that she was living on the South Coast.

That was all I needed. I immediately began thumbing through phone books from the South Coast, looking for the last name France, and within an hour, I was convinced I had found Catherine. But now that I had the information, I felt paralyzed.

"Why don't you call her?" Dan urged. "This is what you've been waiting for."

I looked at him, trying to find the words that would explain the collision of feelings inside me.

"I can't do that yet, Dan," I said finally. "I've got to be at peace with it first."

I headed out for a walk so I could clear my head and get a handle on my emotions. I wanted more than anything to have a relationship with my sister. But now that I knew where she was, I worried how my contacting her would impact her. I remembered what Mrs. Wells had said about her migraines and I didn't want to cause her any more stress.

I kept turning it over in my mind, trying to determine the right thing to do. Though my head warned that contacting her might cause issues, my heart was telling me it was worth the risk. And after hours of walking and thinking, my heart won out.

I headed to the first phone booth I could find, pushed a coin into the slot, and willed my fingers to dial the number I had carefully recorded in the pocket notebook I carried with me.

"Hello?" a woman's voice answered.

I could feel the metal clamps of anxiety tightening against my rib cage. I didn't know why I was so certain, but I knew that voice belonged to my sister.

"I'm sure this comes as a surprise," I said, forcing the words out of my mouth, "but I'm doing research on my family and there's a possibility that we might be related."

The woman paused. I braced myself for her response.

"Are you responding to a newspaper ad?" she asked.

Her question confused me. "Well no," I replied.

"You are my brother, aren't you?" she asked, her voice cracking.

Somewhere amid my shock, I heard myself answer "yes."

"We've been searching for you for the past two years," she said, her excitement and joy so palatable I could feel it through the phone line. "My husband has been placing newspaper ads all over Canada trying to find you."

All my anxiety melted away. I wasn't the only one searching and wanting a relationship. Catherine had been searching for me, too.

In the flurry of excited conversation that followed, Catherine explained that Mrs. Wells had contacted her husband, Jim, shortly after my visit and had told him the entire story—leaving it to him to decide what to do. He had immediately relayed the information to Catherine and the two of them had been searching for me ever since. All they had to go on was my surname and the knowledge that I lived somewhere in Canada. So they had placed newspaper ads in every major city throughout the country.

"I have been praying every day that I would find you," she said. "Finally my prayers have been answered."

Twenty-four hours later, I was sitting in my sister's living room, drinking a celebratory glass of champagne with her and Jim. Though our childhood experiences were as far apart as any could be, there was no denying that we were siblings. I could see my nose and same fine features when I looked at her, and could feel the same indomitable spirit and determination.

Though I told Catherine about the fisherman and his revelation that our mother was now living in New Rochelle, New York, I didn't mention the London incident. It was such a painful memory that I had continued to tell myself it never happened. But as we sat in her living room sipping champagne, Catherine shared her own heartbreaking story of rejection with me.

She told me that she'd spent the first four and a half years of her life living with our grandparents and our Uncle Harry. Though they were poor, Catherine said she was happy and adored her grandfather so much she never wanted to leave his side. Catherine said our mother worked in-service at a wealthy residence in Northern Ireland and came and went. But she said she loved being with her whenever she was home and was always sad when she had to say goodbye. Then one day she was introduced to Mr. and Mrs. Wells, a couple who befriended her and eventually invited her to stay at their house overnight.

"Soon those overnight visits stretched to three and four nights, though they always allowed me to go home whenever I asked," Catherine explained. "And then, without explanation, I was encouraged to keep staying with my new friends by my grandmother."

After a few months, Catherine said Mr. and Mrs. Wells asked her to call them Mummy and Daddy, something she didn't want to do but went along with. Then, she said, they changed her name. Her full name had been Catherine Mary Iris and she had always gone by Iris. But they dropped the other two names and started calling her Catherine.

I could hear the pain in her voice as she shared this with me. My heart felt like it was going to explode as I thought about that little girl whose identity was slowly being stripped from her.

Catherine told me it was during this time that she was walking near the old castle with Mr. and Mrs. Wells and saw our mother sitting on a bench outside the door. Catherine said she was confused and not sure what to do.

"I wanted to run to her and hug her, but wasn't sure if that was the right thing to do because I now had two people I called mummy, and I worried it would make my new one angry if I let go of her hand to run to my own mother," Catherine told me, her voice filled with pain as she recounted the memory. "I was afraid, so I treated her like a stranger and when I looked back, she was gone."

Catherine said she was so crushed by that day it was hard for her to process. She told me she was convinced that it was her fault because she hadn't run to her as she had wanted to do.

Three weeks before World War II started, Catherine said Mr. and Mrs. Wells took her with them to Scotland before eventually settling in England, and she never saw our mother or grandparents again. She said the Wells never talked about her family and she was too afraid to bring them up.

Finally, at the age of twelve, she found the courage to express herself.

"I told them that I wanted to go home," Catherine recounted. "They said that I was home. When I persisted, they told me I couldn't because they had adopted me. Then they told me that my grandmother had written them and asked if they would adopt me."

My gut ached as Catherine wrapped up her story. I wanted to wave a magic wand and take away the intense suffering and depression that had resulted from that rejection and the secrecy surrounding her identity. But I couldn't. All I could do was be grateful that after all of these years, we had found each other.

After sharing stories from our childhood, our conversation shifted to our families now.

We both had three children and I spent a few hours getting acquainted with my two nieces and nephew, and sharing pictures of Ruth and our three children. As we talked, we also discovered we had something else in common: we were both committed Christians.

Given all the miracles that had transpired to get me to this point, I couldn't have envisioned that my reunion with Catherine was just the beginning of the miracles God had in store.

Several years later, upon Mrs. Wells' death, Catherine would donate her adopted mother's estate to Friends in the West—providing the miracle funding necessary to acquire a desperately needed base in both the UK and the United States. Around that same time, her daughter Sally would begin volunteering for the organization and eventually devote her life to the ministry. And amid it all, I would travel back to Culmore Point to inquire about the old fisherman— only to discover that no one in that small village had ever heard of him.

I couldn't have fathomed any of this as I sat in the living room with Catherine and her family, basking in the elation of the moment. The only thought running through my mind was that I was no longer alone. I had a sister who wanted a relationship with me as much as I wanted one with her, and I was one step closer to knowing who I was.

7

January 1977

I KNEW BRITISH PARLIAMENT OFFICIALS were working on the release of Salu Daka Ndebele, a young Christian missionary from Rhodesia (now Zimbabwe) who had been imprisoned in Mozambique for the past year and a half.

But I was still taken back by my friend's pronouncement.

"Ray, I think Salu Daka is out of prison!" Pastor Gary Short exclaimed as he burst into my office.

Gary, who oversaw the Church of Blessed Hope—a small storefront church located in a rundown, gang-riddled section of South Seattle—had become an instrumental part of Friends in the West. His tiny church had gotten behind my organization, providing everything from administrative help to fundraising assistance. Given my complete inability to handle paperwork, write letters, and stay on top of organizational functions, the help that he, his wife, Louise, and their colleague, Suzanne Nelson, provided had become so vital I had recently moved my office to the church and drove the two-and-a-half hour stretch from Canada each Monday to work.

I was confused by Gary's excitement and sudden sense of knowledge about Salu's situation. Though he knew of the missionary's plight and had been praying for him, he hadn't been involved in any of the ongoing talks and efforts to obtain Salu's release.

Before I could ask how he had come to his conclusion, Gary opened his hand and thrust a broken prayer bracelet before me.

"Look at this," he said, motioning to the bracelet that bore Salu's name. "It split in half just a few minutes ago. I think the Lord is telling me that my prayers are answered. I think he's out of prison, Ray."

It was January 1977, fifteen months since I had traveled to Maputo prison in Mozambique to meet with Salu.

His arrest, along with those of Canadian missionary Don Milam, and American missionaries Armand Doll and Hugh Friberg, had come on the heels of the FRELIMO takeover of the country—which had been controlled by Portugal for centuries. FRELIMO, also known as The Mozambique Liberation Front, was a dissident rebel group backed by the Soviet Union. Once in power, the new government had begun locking up anyone who had spoken out against communism or FRELIMO.

I knew it was dangerous going into the country. But I felt I needed to meet with the imprisoned missionaries to let them know I was working on their release and launching a prayer campaign on their behalf.

I had flown into Johannesburg, South Africa, and convinced a young enthusiastic believer, Francis Grim, to make the trek with me. Francis was up for any sort of an adventure. And, as a South African, he knew his way around the political roadblocks.

"If we're going to do this, we've got to head through Swaziland because the South African border is closed," he explained as we planned out our trip. "The Swaziland border may be closed as well, but it's a small local crossing and it's our best shot."

I spent most of the seven-hour drive through the rolling hills, valleys and savannahs lost in my thoughts, trying to devise a plan of action. Though I was concerned about all of the imprisoned Christian missionaries, I was particularly worried about Salu Daka, because unlike the others, he didn't have a Western passport and didn't have powerful government officials working on his release. Salu was a black African from a country that was at odds with Mozambique, which only made his situation worse.

After repeatedly reviewing the problem in my mind, it finally hit me: I would share Salu's story with the media and all of my Friends in the West contacts to generate visibility and international pressure.

"What I'm thinking is that I'll find him in the prison, take a photo of him and then send it out to the press and everyone I know," I told Francis as we drove. "That's got to have an impact."

Francis laughed at my brazenness.

"So how exactly do you think you're going to get a camera into the prison?" he asked.

I smiled and held up the pocket Kodak camera I had brought with me.

"I'll just stick it in my sock," I explained.

Francis didn't have to remind me what would happen if I got caught. I knew it meant joining the other men in prison. But I trusted that God was guiding me and would somehow get me through.

It was late afternoon by the time we reached the border that separated Swaziland from Mozambique. Given the closure of the South African border, we expected to encounter a line of traffic. But there were no other vehicles in sight.

I took a deep breath and whispered a quick prayer in my mind as we drove up to the guard manning the border crossing. He was an old Portuguese man who looked like he had been sleeping and was annoyed at being bothered.

He scowled as his eyes swept over us and rattled off something in Portuguese, which neither of us understood. I grabbed every relevant document I could find in my briefcase and shoved it into the man's hands. It included my Canadian passport, my driver's license and my flight itinerary. Francis followed my lead, handing over his passport and driver's license.

The old man studied our documents without saying anything. I could feel my fingernails digging into my palms as we waited for the border guard's decision.

After a few minutes that felt like hours, he finally handed the documents back to us, muttered something else in Portuguese, and waved us through.

Francis and I both exhaled as we crossed into Mozambique. The first part of our challenge—getting into the country—had been a success.

The streets were eerily quiet as we drove through Maputo, a tropical city lined with trees and historic buildings. We decided to head to an old resort hotel situated on the beach lining the Indian Ocean. The hotel was a worn, old-fashioned facility that looked like it had once been a playground for the wealthy. Usually I wouldn't have even considered staying in a beachfront hotel. But the FRELI-MO takeover had put a virtual halt to tourism and room prices had been slashed so much that they fit within even our modest budget.

As soon as we were situated at the hotel, I arranged a meeting with a local Christian pastor I'd been told about. Given the recent arrests of the other Christians, he was scared for his safety. But he was excited about our visit and mission, and provided us with a rundown of the prison operations.

"You're fortunate because tomorrow is visiting day," he said. "The missionaries should all be out in the prison yard so you shouldn't have any problem meeting with them."

I spent the evening walking the white sandy beach, taking in the shimmery blue water, the stunning rock formations and the endless waves crashing against the shore. I felt so free as I ran my feet through the soft sand and stared out at the seemingly endless body of water. It was hard to imagine that just a few miles away, four Christian missionaries were locked in dark cement cells, uncertain of when they would ever experience the feel of sand on their feet and the endless ocean view.

The following morning it was back to work. I put on a sports jacket, a pair of khaki pants and black knee socks. Then I tucked my camera into the sock so that it sat on the inside of my left calf.

I stood and caught my reflection in the full-length mirror. Staring back at me was a fortyish Caucasian man with a warm smile and sincere eyes framed with glasses. I studied my reflection as though I was a stranger, trying to see what others saw when they looked at me. I was medium height, with a medium build and a studious looking face that seemed to match that of an administrator or college professor. I certainly didn't look the part of someone who was ready to stir the pot and break prison rules.

"Are you ready to do this?" I asked Francis as we sipped our morning tea on the hotel verandah.

Francis grinned.

"Ready," he replied.

Visiting hours were held early afternoon and by the time we arrived at the prison, there was already a long line of friends and loved ones waiting to pass through the imposing iron gate that led to the prison yard.

I said another silent prayer as I waited in line, watching the other visitors being frisked and questioned by the armed guards. I willed my feet to move toward the entrance and concentrated on breathing normally while the prison guard frisked my upper body. I was one of the only Westerners in the entire line and I expected to be grilled on my reasons for being there. But after the brief pat down and standard request to turn over my passport while I was at the prison, I was waved through—my camera still safely tucked inside my sock.

The prison walls were thick and gray and lined with barbed wire and guards with automatic guns. But the large prison courtyard where the visiting hours took place was pleasant enough. It even contained a few tropical shade trees. I scanned the yard and quickly spotted the Canadian and American missionaries. They were standing together in the far left corner.

I could see the questions on their faces as I headed in their direction. I wasn't from their denomination and they had no idea I was coming. But as soon as I introduced myself and explained why I was there, their anxiety turned to hope.

We spent the next few minutes quietly discussing their living situation at the prison and the efforts underway for their release. Along with US and Canadian officials, they told me various members of their denomination were fighting hard to secure their freedom. The men admitted to being down at times, but said their faith was getting them through their ordeal. After a while, our conversation turned to Salu.

"Where is he?" I asked.

One of the men nodded toward a row of cells in the center of the courtyard.

"He's in the first basement cell on the right," he said. "He's so discouraged he didn't bother coming out."

I did a quick scan of the prison yard. Along with the guards at the prison gate, there were several others manning the wall towers that surrounded the yard. But there were at least a hundred inmates and visitors in the courtyard, and I figured they provided me with at least a little bit of a cover.

I said goodbye to the men and casually started walking toward the building that held Salu. As soon as I spotted his cell, I crouched beside the barred window.

"Salu, Salu," I called into the dark cell. "I'm a friend from Canada. Come to the window."

I could see the shock on Salu's face as he made his way toward me.

I quickly introduced myself and explained why I had come.

He looked at me in disbelief.

"You shouldn't be here," he said. "You've got to be very careful or you'll be in here with me."

Salu couldn't have been more than twenty-three, but it was clear that the two and a half months he had spent behind bars was taking its toll. His shoulders slumped as though he was carrying a four hundred pound weight and his face was creased with worry and stress. When he talked, I could hear the hopelessness in his voice.

I wanted to reach through the bars and pull him to freedom. Or at least give him a hug.

I locked my eyes on his so he could see I was serious.

"Salu, I've come to tell you that I will never forget you," I said softly. "I will not stop working on your case until the day you are released."

Salu just shook his head.

"The others will get out," he said. "But that won't happen for me."

His despair was so palpable I could feel it through the steel bars that divided us. It hurt to see someone in such emotional agony.

"Salu, I'm going to help you," I said firmly, once again locking my eyes on his. "I'll start by sharing your picture and story with the world."

Before he could respond, I glanced over my shoulder to make sure no one was watching and then grabbed the camera from my sock.

His expression was a mix of panic and astonishment.

"How did you get that in here?" he asked. "If they catch you, you'll be in here for life."

I smiled, quickly snapped a picture of him and then shoved the camera back into my sock.

"Remember this, Salu," I said as I stood up to leave. "In your darkest hours, no matter how dark they get, I'm here with you. I will never forget you. I will not stop working on your behalf until the day you are released."

I spent a minute mingling among the other visitors and inmates so I didn't stick out, and then slowly headed back to the prison gate. I worried about a post-visit pat down, but the guard just handed me back my passport and pointed me toward the exit. As soon as I was outside the prison wall, I made a beeline for the car, where Francis was waiting.

I felt like singing a doxology. My plan had actually worked. I had done it. With the help of God, I had managed to smuggle in a camera and smuggle out a picture of Salu without being caught.

I didn't have to tell Francis that the mission had been a success. He could see it in the grin that covered most of my face.

"Let's get going before they decide to come after us," I said as I hopped into the car and slammed the front passenger door behind me.

Francis laughed as we pulled out of the prison parking lot.

"I could shimmy up one of those telephone poles and cut the wires so they can't phone the border and stop us," he said, motioning to a utility pole situated on a street just outside of the prison.

I watched his face turn serious and realized he wasn't joking.

"That's okay, Francis," I replied. "God has gotten us this far. I think we'll be fine."

Our next stop was the American Embassy. But when we arrived, we discovered it was closed due to the FRELIMO takeover and uncertainty in the country.

"There's got to be someone inside," I told Francis as I debated what to do. "Let me just check it out."

I walked up to the door and knocked hard. No one answered so I rang the bell and knocked again. Finally a woman opened the door.

She looked surprised to see someone who was clearly from the West.

"We're closed," she said. "But is there something I could help you with?"

I introduced myself and provided a brief overview of the Friends in the West ministry. I also recounted my visit with the imprisoned missionaries.

"I want to do everything I can to help them get released and I figured this was a good starting place," I explained.

The woman invited me to come inside and take a seat in the reception area. Then she disappeared into a back office.

When she returned a few minutes later, she was holding a telex in her hand.

"If I were you, I would start with the new foreign minister, Joaquim Chissano," she said, handing me the telex. "He's going to be leading a delegation to the United Nations soon so that might be a good place to reach him. Here's his itinerary."

I wanted to pinch myself. Once again, it was clear God was guiding me from one stop to the next.

I thanked the woman and then hurried back to the car. Francis and I spent a couple of minutes scanning the foreign minister's itinerary. Sure enough, he was headed to the United Nations—which felt like manna from heaven.

Guy Wiggins had just started to help me take the case of Georgi Vins and the other imprisoned Soviet Christians to Congress and was still wrapping up his post with the United Nations. We had developed a close friendship in the few months since we had met and I knew that if anyone could help me connect with Chissano, it was Guy.

Francis and I immediately headed back across the Swaziland border and into the relative safety of South Africa. As soon as I spotted a phone, I was on a call with Guy—recounting my trip to the prison, my vow to Salu and my stop at the American Embassy that had resulted in the foreign minister's itinerary.

"Chissano is the key in all of this," I explained. 'If we can get him on our side, I think we can get all of the missionaries released."

I heard Guy chuckling from the other end of the line.

"You never stop, do you, Ray? Okay, I'll check into his schedule and see what I can do."

By the time I landed at the United Nations headquarters in New York a week later, Guy had already helped the new foreign minister set up his country's delegation to the United Nations and the two men had formed a friendship. As a result, when Guy introduced me and asked Chissano if he would take a few minutes to meet with me, the foreign minister agreed.

Chissano was a big man with a booming voice and a huge presence. I wasn't sure how he would respond to my request. But he listened politely while I explained my organization's mission to help imprisoned Christians around the world, told him about my visit with the missionaries imprisoned in Mozambique, and asked if there was any way he could assist in getting them released.

I could see a spark of fire flash across the foreign minister's face.

"We'll release the Americans and Canadian," he said finally. "But tell them to mind their own business next time and to stay out of the business of our country."

I understood his anger. I knew that from his point of view, his country had been occupied for centuries and that he and other FRE-LIMO fighters had risked their lives to fight for their freedom. They didn't need outsiders judging or condemning them.

"You're absolutely right," I said. "They do need to stay out of politics and I know that they will from this point forward."

I knew I was dealing with a delicate situation and didn't want to push too hard. But he hadn't said anything about the fate of the fourth Christian prisoner.

"What about Salu Daka?" I pressed.

Chissano looked at me and shook his head.

"That is a different matter and will have to be taken up at a whole different level," he replied.

It took longer than I had hoped, but true to Chissano's word, the Western missionaries were eventually released.

But a year after my visit, nothing had changed for Salu. His prediction was right: the white men with their US and Canadian passports had been freed. But he, a black African, had been left to rot behind bars.

I could see the despair on Salu's face when I closed my eyes at night and could hear the hopelessness in his voice. More than anything, I could hear my promise to him screaming in my mind: *In your darkest hours, no matter how dark they get, I'm here with you. I will never forget you. I will not stop working on your behalf until the day you are released.*

I spent long evenings thinking about Salu's case and turning it over in my mind—trying to identify anything else I could possibly do to help him.

I had distributed his picture and story to the media and had sent it out in mass to everyone on my Friends in the West mailing list. I had also had a thousand prayer bracelets made with his name inscribed on them and had distributed them to Christians throughout the US, Canada and United Kingdom. There were at least a thousand people praying for Salu on a daily basis. But he was still behind bars.

It was three in the morning in late fall when the answer finally hit me. I must have been dreaming about Salu because I woke up with a sudden sense of clarity: I had been thinking about it all wrong.

It was true that Salu was Rhodesian, which was a problem given his country's strained relations with Mozambique. It was also true that Rhodesia was fighting to break away from the British government. But the African country was still considered a British Colony, which meant that Salu was entitled to a British passport and all of the protections that came with it.

As soon as I could scrounge up the funds, I purchased a plane ticket and caught a flight to London, where I met with a couple of influential Christian leaders I knew. They, in turn, introduced me to a few empathetic members of Parliament.

When I laid out Salu's case, handed them the picture I had taken of him in his prison cell and shared my thoughts regarding his entitlement to a British passport, they agreed to pick up his cause and help.

"We're not sure what we can do, but we'll look into it," one of the men had said.

The opportunity came a few weeks later in the form of a levy. As part of an effort to secure relations with the newly formed government of Mozambique, the British government was considering spending several million pounds to rebuild a wharf in Maputo.

"We'll work in a clause that threatens to embargo the bill if Salu is not released," the parliament member assured me.

I knew all of this was underway when Gary burst into my office with this pronouncement. But I hadn't heard anything more from my colleagues in the UK and wasn't sure if they had even succeeded in getting the language attached to the levy. And even if they had, there was no guarantee that the government in Mozambique would accept the deal.

I looked at Gary's broken bracelet, wondering if it really could signify a message from God.

Two days later I received the confirmation call.

"Salu is out," the parliament member told me. "We took the picture you gave us, used it as the photo for his British passport, walked into the prison, and walked out with him yesterday. He's a free man."

Relief flooded through me. I could feel myself smiling as I pictured Salu leaving the prison.

I offered a quiet prayer of thanks as the knowledge of his release continued to sink in. I had kept my word to Salu. I had never forgotten him and had kept fighting for his freedom. And with God's guidance and help, Salu was finally a free man.

8

September 1978

I COULD SENSE THE DANGER as we sipped our tea on the verandah outside Kampala International Hotel, contemplating where to spend the night.

Idi Amin's secret police swarmed the outdoor restaurant—all wearing the trademark dark shades, bell-bottom trousers and platform shoes the dictator's brutal security force had become known for. We could feel their piercing eyes on us; hear their sneers as they motioned in our direction.

"They must have a two-beer ration for lunch," my colleague Ted whispered to me, nodding toward a group of men at the next table who were each nursing two bottles of beer.

"Looks like it," I agreed as I nervously eyed them. "I hope it keeps them occupied."

It was September 1978 and Idi Amin's reign of terror was in full swing throughout Uganda. Ted and I had come to the African country in response to reports that Christians were being beaten, imprisoned and, in some cases, murdered for their faith. Though my main focus was the Soviet Christians, I had felt compelled to travel to Kampala against the advice of nearly everyone I knew to meet with

Christian leaders, find out the truth and see what I could do to help. My friend, Ted, a devout Christian from London who was now living in Kenya, had offered to make the journey with me. But now that we were here, we were both having second thoughts. In addition to the fact that Westerners weren't welcome in the country, we knew no one in Kampala and it was becoming increasingly clear that the hotel wasn't a safe place to stay.

My thoughts jumped to Ruth and the kids. I never told them about the danger my work sometimes entailed because I didn't want them to worry. But I felt a void whenever I was away from them. They needed me and I needed them and I knew I would never forgive myself if something happened to me.

By the time we had finished our tea and eaten lunch, the uneasiness swirling inside me had reached a boiling point. The secret police—known as members of the State Research Bureau—continued to surround us and I could feel the tension in the air.

"We've got to get out of here while we still can," I quietly told Ted.

We paid our bill, grabbed our briefcases and shoulder bags, and tried to act unconcerned as we wandered toward the line of taxies. We scanned the drivers before flagging down a man who, at least from a dress perspective, appeared unlikely to be a member of the secret security force.

"We need to get to a guest house near Namirembe Cathedral," I explained to the driver, careful not to mention the word 'Christian'. "Can you take us there?"

The driver, who spoke limited English, nodded and headed across town. We were relieved to get away from the hotel. But when he stopped a few minutes later, we were nowhere near the cathedral. We were in front of a rundown building that turned out to be a Muslim guest house near the mosque.

"No, no, this is the wrong place," I said, swallowing the panic that was shooting through me. "We need to go to the Namirembe Cathedral."

I felt light-headed and dizzy as my anxiety and stress took hold. Dusk was settling in and the city was under strict curfew. People disappeared at night on a regular basis—and being white only increased the danger. We had to get off the streets.

Our driver headed back across town and slowed down as he neared the cathedral. I had been told that the guest house was somewhere close, but I couldn't see anything that gave it away.

I could feel the driver's uneasiness and knew he wanted us out of his cab. I whispered a silent prayer and, as if on cue, I spotted a young woman who looked to be in her early twenties walking down a hill toward us. My heart leaped when I saw the Bible tucked under her arm.

I asked the cab driver to stop and quickly hopped out of the car.

"Excuse me," I said, hoping that she could understand English. "We're looking for a Christian guest house but I'm afraid we're lost. Do you by chance know where it is?"

A large smile broke open across her face.

"Yes," she said, her voice brimming with excitement. "It's run by friends of mine. I'll take you there.

"I can't believe this," she added. "We were just praying for someone from the West to come."

I was so relieved and grateful to have found someone who could help us that the last part of her sentence didn't register. We paid the cab driver and then waited until he was gone before following the girl to a modest whitewashed guest house tucked against the hill in the shadows of the cathedral.

"My name is Faith," she said as we walked toward the guest house.

The irony in that particular moment, given the complete leap of faith I had taken to get to this point, was so strong I couldn't help but smile.

Yeah, and I'm Pilgrim, I wanted to reply.

There was a buzz of excitement among the guest house staff as Faith introduced Ted and me and explained that we needed a place to stay. I didn't understand why everyone seemed so jubilant until I started talking with Stephen Gonahassa, who ran the guest house with his wife, Naomi.

I began the conversation by explaining that I operated a small Christian-based organization that helped shine the spotlight on suffering Christians around the world, and had come to Uganda to find out what had really happened to a congregation of believers from the Makerere Full Gospel Church, whom I had been told had been arrested and imprisoned a few months earlier.

Stephen's eyes immediately flooded with tears.

"We just prayed specifically that the Lord would allow someone to come from the West to visit us," he explained, repeating the story Faith had told us. "We asked Him to do this so we'd know He hadn't forgotten His Ugandan church. Surely the Lord has sent you."

I was stunned, especially when Stephen told me that no Westerners had stopped by the guest house in some time. But then I felt a quiet sense of calm and purpose wash over me. Stephen's revelation confirmed what I already knew: that God had guided me here.

"Would it be possible to make contact with some of the Christian leaders?" I asked.

Stephen smiled. "Word is already on the way," he replied. "You must be patient, though, because we do not have gasoline for cars, so messages must be taken by bicycle or on foot."

Within an hour Ben Oluka, a leader in the underground church who also happened to work in church relations in President Amin's cabinet, showed up at the guest house. I told him about the Friends in the West mission and then jumped directly to the incident that had driven me to make the journey.

"Is it true," I asked, "that an entire congregation was imprisoned last Easter?"

"Yes," Ben responded quietly. "They were held, beaten, deprived of food and threatened with death for three months."

I could hear the pain in his voice as he spoke. I had been told of the incident by a woman who attended Glad Tidings Church in Vancouver, but I needed to know more.

"Would it be possible to meet with the pastor from the church?" I asked.

"I think we can arrange this," Ben replied. "We are in very close fellowship."

The next morning, Ben showed up at the guest house in a black limousine—which I later learned was from Idi Amin's personal fleet of cars—to take Ted and me to an underground church in the outskirts of Kampala.

The limo dropped us in front of a house where furniture was made, which served as a front for the church. The back door of the cottage led to a banana grove. And behind the banana grove stood the house that held the secret meetings.

Despite the danger, I couldn't help but smile as I made my way through the secret passageway. Even from the road, I could hear the beautiful voices of joyful Christians singing the hymn, *Our God Reigns*.

Like Stephen, the believers who risked their safety to come together for worship were moved to tears when they saw Ted and me, and heard about our mission. We spent hours after the service talking with members of the congregation and listening as they recounted the ongoing struggles and persecution they faced. While there, we were introduced to Jotham Mutebi, the assistant pastor who had led the Easter service at Makerere Church in Kampala that terrifying Sunday five months earlier.

Pastor Mutebi told us that the church had been closed by authorities, but said that he and the other leaders had decided to reopen it and were in the middle of worship when the attack began.

"The church was surrounded by soldiers wearing full battle dress," Pastor Mutebi said. "They were armed with automatic weapons and even had a machine gun. We were shocked when they stormed into the church and began firing their automatic guns into the congregation."

Pastor Mutebi, who was on the platform, told us he sank to his knees in prayer and said that the congregation followed. Then, said Mutebi, the church trumpeter grabbed his horn and blew it as loud as he could. The soldiers, confused and scared, stopped firing and retreated from the church. But minutes later, Mutebi said they were back in the church, shooting into the walls and smashing instruments. He said the soldiers then rounded up the entire congregation, forced them outside by gunpoint and made them lay in piles on top of one another while they kicked and beat them.

"The very old and very young were weeded out, but about two hundred believers were forced into lorries and rushed off to prison," Pastor Mutebi continued, his body tensing as he recounted the incident. "I knew this could be the end because most people never left the prison alive. When we arrived at the prison, the other leaders and I were separated and beaten without mercy."

While he and the other leaders were being assaulted and interrogated, Pastor Mutebi told us the rest of the believers were kept outside and ordered to sit on the ground in a circle, where they were told that gasoline would be poured on them and they would be burned alive.

The soldiers taunted and beat the believers while they waited for the death order to be signed by Vice President Mustafa Adrisi, who had ordered the raid on the church. But in an instant, said Pastor Mutebi, everything changed. While en route to his office, the vice president was involved in a high-speed head-on collision and suffered such serious injuries that he was flown to Cairo for treatment.

"The soldiers held them at gunpoint for several hours," Pastor Mutebi recounted. "But when the signed death order never came, the congregation was herded into the prison and placed in dark, cramped cells."

For the next two months, Pastor Mutebi said he and his five fellow church leaders—who were eventually transferred to the central police station—suffered continuous harassment and torture. Pastor Mutebi told us he was burned on the face with cigarettes and once had a guard try to break his wrist. And he said the beatings were relentless.

"We would be lined up and made to squat. Then a policeman would come down the line and beat each of us with a stick," he said. "One day, an officer split open my head with an iron bar as I squatted there."

The two hundred members of the congregation, who were being held at the Luzira maximum-security prison, were also enduring constant beatings and harassment. While there, said Pastor Mutebi, other prisoners were taken away and shot, and the believers didn't know if each day would be their last. They were stuffed into severely overcrowded cells and were sometimes forced to go without food.

But through it all, he said they held strong in their faith—even praying for their captors.

"Then God intervened again," the pastor told us. "On May 28th, I was released with the other church leaders without explanation. One month later, on June 30th, the remaining church members were released. Miraculously, no one died."

I sat on the verandah of the guest house a few days later, reflecting on the story Pastor Mutebi had told me and everything I had learned since arriving in Uganda—the persecution, the miracles, and the perseverance, faith and joy the Ugandan Christians displayed amid their suffering. I was particularly struck by their courage. During the course of the week, I had met several influential Christian leaders. A few, like Ben, worked in Idi Amin's presidential office and engaged in a dangerous balancing act—utilizing their position and the information gained to help the Christian community. Others worked in banking and education and also leveraged their positions to help in any way possible.

I had established numerous contacts and had made friendships that I knew would last well into the future. I felt like I had accomplished what I had come to Uganda to do: I had found out the truth about the situation facing the Ugandan Christians and had given them a voice that I would make sure was heard throughout the Western world. I had also provided them with hope by letting the believers know that people in the West cared about them and that they weren't alone.

I felt good about my Uganda trip. But there was another matter pressing on my mind: the ongoing plight of Pastor Georgi Vins. It had been two years since the passage of the Congressional Resolution that condemned the Soviet Union for its persecution of Christians and demanded the release of the Baptist pastor. Yet nothing had changed for him. Georgi Vins was still being tortured and starved in the Siberian Gulags and I'd heard reports that his mother and son had also been arrested. My contacts behind the Iron Curtain warned that the pastor's health was failing and urged me to step up efforts to get him released before it was too late.

My heart was heavy as I thought about the pastor. I had been working hard for three and a half years to secure his release and hadn't been able to do anything to help him.

As I looked out over the city of Kampala, racking my mind for answers, I suddenly remembered a *Readers Digest* story I had read during a flight a couple of years earlier. It was the story of American U-2 spy plane pilot Gary Francis Powers, who had been captured by the Soviets. The story—which decades later would be captured in the film *Bridge of Spies* starring Tom Hanks—spotlighted Wolfgang Vogel, a famous lawyer in East Berlin who worked as a mediator between Moscow and Washington D.C. and had negotiated the swap of Powers for a master soviet spy who had been captured in the United States. The *Readers Digest* story also mentioned other political prisoner swaps Mr. Vogel had orchestrated.

I felt a sudden volt of energy charging through me. I had often thought about seeking out the attorney's help. Now I was feeling that intense pull inside of me and knew it was the right time.

My mind began racing. Ted and I were scheduled to leave Kampala the following day. After a stop in Nairobi where Ted and I initiated our journey, my flight routed me through London, where I had a three-day layover before flying home to Canada. I realized it would be easy to make a quick trip from London to Berlin to meet up with

Mr. Vogel. The only problem was that I had no money for the airfare.

Friends in the West was running on fumes and I had barely managed to scrape together the funding to get to Kampala. There were no extra funds to get me to Berlin.

I spent the next fifteen minutes turning the problem over in my mind. Then it hit me: I had a camera I could sell.

My Praktica camera, which had been given to me as a gift, was one of the only items of value I owned. I always took it with me when I traveled so I could capture photos to share with the Friends in the West community. But now I realized it could provide the means to help get Georgi Vins released.

I had seen a couple of the wealthy Ugandan businessmen who were staying at the guest house eyeing the camera when I had it out before, and decided they were my best shot. I waited until one of them joined me on the verandah with his morning cup of tea and then took my camera out of its case and began snapping photos, commenting loudly on the beauty of the pictures I was capturing.

It was all a ruse. I didn't even have film in the camera. But I could see out of the corner of my eye that the businessman was watching.

I continued snapping photos, dramatically turning my camera to get different angles.

"That looks like a great camera," the Ugandan businessman said finally.

I turned to him and smiled.

"Oh yes," I said, "It is a great camera. It was expensive but it's worth it because it takes beautiful pictures."

I could see him salivating. I knew they didn't sell cameras like these in Uganda.

"Would you be interested in selling it?" he asked. "I'd like to purchase it."

I didn't say anything for a minute, hoping he would take my silence as hesitation.

"It's hard to part with it," I said finally. "But I know you will love this and I can always purchase another one."

Within minutes we had negotiated a deal for the camera and I had the money I needed to get to Berlin. Later that afternoon, one of my new friends who worked at the bank converted the Ugandan shillings into British pounds for me and I was on my way.

I landed in West Berlin on an early Sunday afternoon and headed to a bed and breakfast to check in for the night. I had no idea how to go about getting a hold of Wolfgang Vogel and wasn't at all sure of what I was getting myself into. I didn't even know if he was still living in East Berlin and for all I knew, he could have been a KGB agent himself. But something inside of me was pushing me toward him. Regardless of the outcome, I knew I had to find out if Mr. Vogel could help me.

I decided to head to a Sunday evening service at a nearby Christian church someone had recommended, figuring someone there might be able to assist me.

As soon as the service ended, the young pastor who had delivered the sermon made a beeline for me.

"Pastor Barnett, what a wonderful surprise!" he exclaimed in excited broken English. "I heard you preach in Dusseldorf when I was sixteen years old and I've never forgotten you."

I smiled, feeling the same calm and sense of purpose that I had experienced in Kampala. I knew it wasn't a coincidence that I had ended up at this church with this pastor.

We spent a few minutes talking about the pastor's decision to go into the ministry. Then I explained why I had come to Berlin and asked if he had any ideas for how to connect with the attorney.

"I know the man who runs the Berlitz School,"he replied. "He's involved in these types of things and will be able to help you."

The next morning I received a call from Pierre Witzmann, the director for the international language school. He said he would contact Mr. Vogel on my behalf, and even offered to serve as my interpreter. Within an hour, he called again, telling me that arrangements had been made.

"He said we can come today,"Pierre told me. "We just have to be there before 3 p.m. because he is leaving for a trip and won't be available after that."

I could feel myself smiling. It was all coming together.

The previous evening, the pastor had introduced me to a member of his congregation who worked for *Time* magazine's West Berlin bureau chief. She had offered to dig up a small article the magazine had run about Georgi Vins and his plight in the Siberian labor camp and had delivered it to where I was staying. On a whim, I also grabbed the copy of the Congressional Resolution I always carried with me and tucked it into my suit pocket.

At noon, Pierre and I boarded the U-Bahn that took us through an underground tunnel to Soviet-controlled East Berlin. We spent an hour and a half navigating the tight security checkpoints, and when we finally emerged from Friedrichstrasse U-Bahn station, it was nearly 2 p.m.

Everything around me felt heavy, grey and tense. Though we had only crossed to the other side of the city, it felt like we had stepped onto another planet. The buildings were drab, colorless and rundown, matching the seemingly sullen moods of everyone we saw.

We rushed to the nearest street corner to flag down a taxi, figuring that it would be easy to find a cab outside of the train station. But there were none to be found.

I could feel my body heating up as my anxiety took over. Wolfgang Vogel lived in the outskirts of the city, much too far to travel to by foot. And the clock was ticking.

We stood at the corner, silently begging and praying for a taxi to land.

Ten minutes past, then twenty.

I checked my watch eve[ry minute or anything else to see]. Mr. Vogel had made it clear t[hat we had to be there by 3 p.m. What] if we didn't make it?

Another agonizing fiftee[n] minutes past. Finally, at 2:55 p.m., a taxi pulled up to the curb.

"Tell him we've got to ge[t there fast," I urged Pierre as we heap]ed ourselves into the back sea[t.]

We sped through town [and pulled up to a large brick house in] the suburbs of East Berlin wi[th five minutes to spare. I worried that] Mr. Vogel would tell us we we[re too late and turn us away. But when] we knocked on the door of [the elegant home, a studious-looking] woman invited us in and instr[ucted us to take a seat in the most clas]sically beautiful office I had e[ver encountered.]

Books lined the warmly p[ainted walls and a plush rug covered] the rich hardwood floors. A large cherry oak desk sat near one end of the room, surrounded by several intricate antique pieces.

After a few moments, Mr. Vogel entered the room. He was a tall, distinguished-looking man with silver hair and a serious demeanor. But I could see sincerity in his eyes.

I apologized for arriving so late, thanked him for meeting with me on such short notice and then quickly launched into my reason for being there.

"I run a small nonprofit organization that helps persecuted and imprisoned Christians," I started, keeping my eyes trained on his. "I read about you in a *Readers Digest* story about Gary Francis Powers and came to you in hopes that you could help secure the release of Pastor Georgi Vins."

I had assumed that he knew all about the pastor and his plight. But as Pierre translated my words, I could see a blank look on Mr. Vogel's face.

"Here," I said, pulling out the *Time* story and laying it before him on his desk. "This is the man I've come to see you about. He's spent the past three and a half years in a Siberian labor camp because of his faith."

Mr. Vogel studied the article while Pierre translated.

"This is interesting," he said finally. "I've been visited by numerous Jewish delegations. But I've never had someone come to me on behalf of Christians before."

His words surprised me. Given how many Christian leaders had been imprisoned in the Soviet Union and the broad-spread awareness of their suffering, it seemed like others would have thought of coming to Mr. Vogel on their behalf.

It was becoming clear that the attorney didn't waste words because for a while, he didn't say anything. But he kept studying the *Time* story in front of him and I got the sense that he was moved by Pastor Vins' plight.

"What you ask could be very dangerous for him," Mr. Vogel said finally, looking at me intently.

I took this as my opening.

"I don't think it could get much worse," I replied returning his gaze while Pierre translated. "His son and mother have also been imprisoned for their faith and Pastor Vins is very ill. It's already a very dangerous situation."

We had been in the meeting for more than twenty minutes and I saw Mr. Vogel glancing at his watch. I knew our time was nearly up.

He looked at the *Time* story again and then back up at me.

"Do you have anything else?" he asked.

Between the stress of making it to the meeting on time and the intensity of the conversation, I had forgotten all about the Congressional Resolution.

I reached into my suit pocket, pulled it out and unfolded it.

"I have this," I said, handing him the sheet of paper.

I could see Mr. Vogel's expression change the minute his eyes locked on the document. He listened intently as my colleague translated the Resolution for him, and I watched his mouth turn into a half smile.

I wondered if he thought I was somehow connected with the US government and had been sent on the government's behalf. I'd never put much weight in the Congressional Resolution. But as he continued to stare at the document, I realized that I had given him a valuable piece of information because it told him that Georgi Vins was important to the United States government.

I immediately recognized what he was thinking: that he could use this as a bargaining chip.

Bolstered by his increased interest in Georgi Vins, I jumped to the other issue on my agenda: the case of a group of Pentecostals, dubbed the Siberian Seven, who had made a dash for the American Embassy in Moscow and had already been self-imprisoned there for sixty days.

But this time, when Pierre translated my words, Mr. Vogel shook his head.

"This isn't the right time for that," he said, walking toward his office door to signal that our meeting was over. "But I will look into the other matter. I have your contact details."

I was working in my Seattle office a few months later when his letter arrived. It was a short note scrawled in German and I immediately took it to Suzanne Nelson for help.

Suzanne, a smart, talented woman in her mid-twenties who had started the Church of Blessed Hope with Gary and Louise Short, had become my counterpart. She had been so moved by the Friends in the West mission to help persecuted Christians that she had started donating her day off each week to help me. While I drove the vision for the organization, Suzanne handled the organizational and administrative functions necessary to keep Friends in the West afloat.

Suzanne's grandfather happened to be from Germany and she immediately drove the letter to his house for translation.

Like at our meeting in East Berlin, Wolfgang Vogel didn't waste words in his note.

"Mr. Barnett, what you ask is very difficult," the letter read. *"But please be assured, I'm attending to it."*

I felt a sense of peace wash over me as Suzanne read his translated letter over the phone. I didn't know when Georgi Vins would be released. But for the first time in the four years I had been pushing in every direction I could think of to help secure his freedom, I felt that progress was being made.

I was driving the weekly trek between Vancouver and Seattle four months later when the news report came over the radio. I was so stunned as I listened to the words I nearly crashed into the car in front of me.

Baptist dissident Georgi Vins has just arrived in Washington D.C. His plane touched down at Dulles Airport moments ago. Forty-eight hours before he had been in a Siberian transport train, on his way to a labor camp. This morning he will have breakfast with President Jimmy Carter. Vins' release was arranged by East German attorney Wolfgang Vogel. The well-known prisoner was exchanged to the west for two KGB agents.

I pulled off the freeway at the next exit and stopped in a nearby fast food parking lot so I could process the news I had just heard.

It was late April 1979, more than four years since Georgi Vins had been arrested and sentenced to hard labor in the Siberian Gulags. After all the years of praying, prodding and pleading for the pastor's release, God—working through Wolfgang Vogel—had made it happen.

As I sat in that parking lot reveling in the joy and knowledge that Pastor Georgi Vins was finally a free man, I realized that while it had been a long journey, none of my efforts had been a waste.

As in so many other situations in my life, God had guided me from one necessary step to the other, with the Congressional Resolution serving as a key piece of the puzzle even when I couldn't see how it fit. It was a reminder of how faith and prayer worked: I didn't have to know the big picture. I just had to trust God's guidance and keep moving forward.

9

June 1982

IMAGES OF BOMBED-OUT BUILDINGS, mountains of rubble and crying children flashed across my TV screen as Ted Koppel reported on the dire situation in Lebanon.

It was June 1982, and Israel, fed up with constant attacks by the Palestinian Liberation Organization, had invaded Lebanon in an effort to eliminate the rebel group from the country. According to the Nightline news report, the massive Israeli attacks were coming from both air and sea—preventing ships from delivering desperately needed food and medical supplies to people living in the ancient coastal cities of Sidon and Tyre.

I stared at my television screen, wondering why no one was stepping in to help. The crisis didn't make sense to me. If the ports were being blocked, why wasn't food and medical aid being delivered over land behind the Israeli forces?

My mind raced as I thought about ways I could help. During my years in the travel agency business, I had spent some time working for the Israeli airline El Al, arranging faith-based trips to the holy sites. As a result, I knew my way around the region and knew I could be of assistance.

The problem, as always, was money. Friends in the West was so broke that just two days earlier, Suzanne—who was now devoting most of her time to the organization—had proposed getting an outside job.

"I'll still find time to help out," she explained. "We just need some money coming in to pay the bills."

Her words were distressing. What was wrong with me that I couldn't manage to drive in the necessary funding to keep the ministry going? I didn't want Suzanne working double shifts just so that she could keep us afloat. It wasn't right.

I could feel the despair swirling inside me as the weight of her words sunk in. Without Suzanne, I didn't know how I could keep the organization running.

"You shouldn't have to do that," I told her. "I'll figure something out. You're needed here and if God wants us to keep doing this work, he'll supply the money."

I spent the night staring at my bedroom ceiling as images of hungry, crying children and their battered, desperate mothers flashed repeatedly through my mind. I could feel the familiar pull inside of me and knew I had to get involved. But then my thoughts jumped back to the conversation with Suzanne. How was I possibly going to launch a relief effort in Lebanon when I couldn't even cover our meager operating costs?

It was nearly 5 a.m. when the idea began forming in my mind: I could approach a well-funded nonprofit Christian organization based in Los Angeles. The organization operated a Christian radio station out of Lebanon near the border of Israel—which made it a natural fit for the relief effort. I was acquainted with George Otis, the president of the organization, and one of my board members and closest friends, Jerry Jensen, served on their board. It seemed like a good possibility.

I felt bad leaving my family again. I wasn't even sure how I was going to provide for them while I was gone. I knew that my chosen ministry meant that they had to make continued sacrifices and it hurt. But Ruth had watched me agonize through the night and knew that I had to do what I could to help.

"We'll be fine," she assured me. "Just do what you need to do. Somehow, God will provide."

I packed my suitcase, said my goodbyes to Ruth, Rob, Rheanne and Rhonda, and climbed into my beat-up yellow Nissan to make the twenty-hour trek to Southern California. Driving was my only option because aside from a gas credit card, all of my credit cards were maxed out.

As I drove, I thought about what I could possibly say that would convince George to fund the mission. I knew it was going to be a tough sell because in addition to asking for a large chunk of money, I was asking an evangelical Christian organization to help a largely Muslim community. But as I saw it, being a devoted Christian meant helping anyone in need, regardless of religious beliefs.

Jerry arranged a meeting with George, who greeted me warmly and listened politely as I told him about my desire to launch a food and medical aid mission in Lebanon and my need for funding. But I could sense from his body language and the growing frown on his face that he wasn't interested.

"We can't help you with that," he said when I finished talking. "It would be too expensive and we don't have any experience with that sort of thing. We're in the process of building a peace chapel in the strip between Israel and Lebanon so there's a place where people from both sides can worship."

I wasn't sure whether to laugh or scream at the ridiculousness of what I was hearing. Had he not heard the news reports and seen the images?

"George, in normal circumstances that's a great idea but they don't need a peace chapel right now," I replied, fighting to keep the frustration out of my voice. "The entire country is at war and people are starving and in pain. What they need is food and medicine."

George reiterated his position and showed Jerry and me to the door. I could see the embarrassment on Jerry's face as we headed back to his car.

"I'm sorry, Ray," he said. "I thought George would be more open to the idea."

I was exhausted from my drive and discouraged that the meeting hadn't gone as I had hoped. But I knew God was guiding me toward Lebanon and one way or another, I was going to find the money to make the mission possible.

I sat in silence in the car, racking my brain for answers. I was in California, where there was plenty of money. I just had to find someone willing to help me. I had a contact in San Diego and decided to head there next.

"It's okay, Jerry," I replied. "If you just drop me at the train station, I'll make a quick trip to San Diego and see if I can find some help there.

"But I wouldn't be surprised if George calls you to say he's changed his mind," I added.

I wasn't sure why that thought popped into my mind. But I knew George was a caring, devoted man and that his organization was a perfect fit for the Lebanese aid mission. I was so hopeful that he would have a change of heart that I called Jerry from the train station payphone as soon as I landed in San Diego.

He answered on the first ring. "Ray, you were right," he said, his voice bursting over the phone line. "George just called and wants to meet again. Can you catch the train back? We've got to meet first thing in the morning because he's heading out on vacation."

I could hear the relief in his voice when he spoke and could feel it rushing through me as I boarded the return train to Los Angeles.

When I saw George again, it was a night and day difference.

"Okay, I'll do it," he said as soon as we were seated in his office. "How much do you need to cover Friends in the West operating costs while you are gone?"

I was so surprised by his complete turnaround that for a minute I couldn't think. When I finally suggested a $5,000 monthly budget, he didn't blink.

"Fine," George replied, "we'll cover that. We'll also give you $5,000 for seed money to purchase food and medical supplies, and will provide you with an American Express credit card to cover your personal expenses there. We'll also give you use of our van."

Just like that, all of the roadblocks were gone. It was as though God had personally placed the order and had written out a check on my behalf.

I could feel Suzanne's joy through the phone line when I called to tell her the news.

"I knew God would take care of things," I said, feeling myself smiling as I spoke. "We just have to keep going and have faith.

"Could I ask a favor?" I added. "If I purchase an airplane ticket for you, will you fly down here and drive back my car for Ruth? I'm flying out tonight."

I hung up the phone with Suzanne and called Ruth to share the news and tell her the plan. Like Suzanne, I could hear the relief in her voice when she spoke.

"I knew God would provide," she said. "Go and do what you

need to do."

↜

Thirty-six hours later I was in the Israeli border town of Metula, standing in the office of the commanding general who was overseeing the military operation.

Obtaining permission to move freely between the two countries was a crucial first step in my mission. But the general was shaking his head before I even finished making my request.

"Absolutely not," he replied in a sharp, exasperated tone. "I can't let you go in there. I don't have people to protect you. Journalists can't even go in there."

The general looked tired and strained, reflecting my stress and exhaustion. I didn't know how I was possibly going to get access into the Lebanon war zone, but it was clear I would have to find another way.

I thanked him for his time and moved toward the door.

"Mr. Ray, why do you want to go there?" the general called after me.

I whispered a quick thank you prayer in my mind as I turned back to address him.

"Thousands of Lebanese families are starving and suffering because of the invasion," I said, eyeing him steadily. "I'd like to start a relief effort to help them."

I quickly told the general about the Ted Koppel news report, my background as a minister and president of Friends in the West, and my plan to launch a food and medical relief effort to help the Lebanese people.

"I know Israel hasn't done this on purpose," I said, wrapping up my pitch, "but all the world sees is that thousands of innocent civilians are suffering and that ships can't get food and medical supplies to them. If we could get aid in there via land through Haifa, I think it would be great PR for Israel."

The general stared at me for a minute. Then he reached into his pocket, pulled out a passbook, and ripped out a border-crossing pass.

"I can't provide any security," he said as he handed me what amounted to a golden ticket. "You're on your own."

I was so stunned by the complete turnaround that it took me a minute to react.

"I understand completely," I finally replied, tucking the pass into my pocket before he changed his mind. "Thank you."

I left the general's office and headed to the only hotel in town. Then I took a seat in the lobby to contemplate my next move.

My first big hurdle—getting access between Israel and Lebanon—was out of the way. But now came the hard part: I had to find a place to set up a base, figure out where to purchase food and medical supplies, and assemble a team of volunteers willing to help me.

I listened as gunshots and mortar fire erupted across the border and felt the first twinges of worry and doubt settling in. I had been so determined to get here and start helping the trapped civilians that I hadn't spent any time considering the enormity of the task ahead. The answer had seemed obvious when I watched the terror unfold on my TV screen from the safety of my living room at home. But now that I was actually in the middle of the war zone, kicking off a food and medical relief effort didn't look so easy. I'd never launched a relief effort before and had no idea what was entailed. On top of that, I had only $5,000 in seed money and the use of a van. It was like feeding the five thousand with a few loaves of bread and a couple of fish. How was I going to possibly turn $5,000 and a van into a sustainable operation?

I could feel anxiety taking over and was so exhausted that I decided to head to my room for some sleep. But just as I was about to leave, a child's voice stopped me.

"Excuse me, mister. Are you American?"

I looked down to see a young girl with dark hair and chocolate eyes staring up at me.

"No dear," I replied. "I'm just a Canadian."

Her face lit up.

"Oh that's very good," she said, her broken English laced with a strong French accent. "I'm from Lebanon. My family is staying with my grandparents just across the border and we have come here to phone my auntie in Montreal.

"My name is Jane," the girl added. "I'm ten."

Despite my exhaustion and worry, I felt myself smiling. Jane had such a vivacious perso_____ _____ _____ breath of fresh air amid the gloom of the ___ raging around us.

Her father, who ___ been standing nearby, joined our conversation. He introduced himself as Professor Kheirla and told me he taught at the evangeli___ ____ school in Sidon.

"We've been stay___ with my wife's parents across the border in the safe zone ever sin___ _____," he explained.

I could hear the _____ __ his voice. That's when I introduced myself and told him v___ I was here. "I will help find some for God," I said.

"We'll help you, _____ Kheirla said. "My wife, Karima, is the president of the YW___ and my son, Rashid, is an Eagle Scout. If you help us clean up _____, you can sleep at your base."

Once again, Gc___ ___ stepped in to help.

I drove Professor Kheirla and his daughter across the border to his in-laws house—situated in the free zone operated by Colonial

Hadad, a Lebanese Christian—that evening, where I met Kathy and Ronnie. I was back the following morning to pick up my new friends and drive into Sidon.

It was only a half-hour drive to the coastal city. But it felt like we had entered another planet.

My heart sank as I took in the devastation. Sidon, known for its beautiful ancient architecture and historic buildings, was now a pile of rubble. Mounds of debris lined the streets, and the air was so clogged with thick cement dust it was difficult to breathe.

Groups of people huddled outside of bombed out homes, using water and strips of clothing to clean and dress each other's wounds. The scene repeated itself block after block. There was no way to escape the children begging for food, or the heavy gloom that permeated the city.

I could feel despair setting in. I knew I was where God wanted me, but I was overwhelmed by the enormity of the challenge.

We arrived at the Kherela house, located on one of the main streets in the city, and silently began sweeping up the shattered glass and clumps of plaster that covered the floors and furniture. Once done, we gathered in the living room to map out a strategy.

I didn't know where to begin. But Kathy immediately jumped in with an idea.

"There's an orphanage on top of the hill that's run by nuns," she said. "I don't know what the situation is like, but I think that would be a good place to start."

Ronnie reached out to friends in the community and within an hour, we had tracked down a half-ton each of flour, sugar and rice that we purchased with some of the seed money I had been given.

I expected to encounter hungry children at the orphanage. Instead, we walked into a makeshift refugee camp. The place was so crammed with people it was hard to move. I could feel the despair in the air and see it on the jumbled faces of mothers, children and elderly women and men.

When the nuns saw the food, their eyes brimmed with tears. They told me they had been praying for help, and for a way to feed the people.

And with that, Operation Lebanon Aid was officially underway.

The Kherelas offered me a bedroom in their home to use as my Sidon base and began introducing me to both Christian and Muslim families in the community. Chuck Pollack, who managed the radio station run by the organization that had made the aid mission possible, also began introducing me to key people.

Word spread fast and requests for help began pouring in. The first came from a woman who lived next door to my new friends. She explained that her visiting niece had diabetes and was out of insulin.

"Can you help us?" she pleaded.

I assured the woman I would take care of it and drove into Israel the following morning to purchase the medication. When I stopped by the house to deliver the insulin later that day, I learned that the girl, Bahesiah, was from Egypt and had been visiting her aunt when the fighting erupted.

"She's been trapped here ever since and we don't have a way to get her home," her aunt confided. "Her parents have passed away but she lives with an older brother and has a happy life there."

I was immediately taken with Bahesiah. She was a beautiful, spirited eleven-year-old girl who longed to return home, but was petrified of the Israelis. When I told her I was going to personally obtain the airline ticket for her and escort her to the Tel Aviv airport, she panicked.

"But Mr. Ray, the Israelis will slit my throat!" she bellowed.

She calmed down after I explained to her that the Israeli people meant no harm to her and that I would personally make sure she safely got on the plane. By the time I made contact with her brother and got her to the airport a week later, she had much more pressing issues on her mind.

"Mr. Ray, is this a first-class ticket?" she asked.

I couldn't help but smile. "No Bahesiah, but it will get you home," I replied.

Bahesiah's aunt turned out to be well connected in the Muslim con   heart medica-
tior   own in Israel
and   ved as prime
mir

                                                                        ded that they
joir   deliver food
anc   a fundraiser
for   Pollack, who
hac   the Lebanon
Ai   tian radio sta-
tio   began arriving
in

                                                                        n. He told me
that an Israeli colonial he worked with had been concerned about the humanitarian crisis facing the Lebanese civilians and was impressed with the work I had been doing in Sidon.

"I know you need volunteers to help you," he said as he pulled out his passbook and handed it to me. "So you sign and I'll counter-sign."

Despite my lack of organizational skills, I was soon running a large, coordinated relief effort that included issuing passes for volun-

teers, finding housing for them, and establishing work teams to facilitate the purchase, packaging and delivery of supplies through Sidon
and Tyre. I also oversaw the medical teams, taking them into the war
zones along the coast to tend to the sick and injured.

One of the first medical teams to arrive was a female doctor and
nurse team from Finland. The women were passionate about their
work. The historical sites in the region also fascinated them. One
late afternoon as we wrapped up their traveling clinic for the day and
were on our way back to Metula, the women asked if I would take
them to Beaufort Castle, an ancient castle in Southern Lebanon that
overlooked Israel.

It was nearly dusk by the time we parked and walked the twenty
yards to the castle lookout point. We spent a few minutes in silence,
taking in the beauty of the city lights and views below. I was so engrossed in the view that at first Petra's words didn't register.

"Ray, don't you think they're shooting at us?" she asked, pointing to the large rock situated five feet in front of us.

Just then I heard a small ping and saw a bullet ricochet off the
rock. Another one followed, then another.

"Yeah, I think you're right," I responded.

"What do you think we should do?"

I could hear the panic in Petra's voice and could feel it worming
its way through my body as the reality of our situation sunk in.

The bullets were now hitting every few seconds. It was only a
matter of time before one of us would be hit.

"I think we should duck behind that rock," I said, concentrating
on keeping my voice calm.

The three of us crouched to the ground and inched our way to
the shelter provided by the boulder in front of us, bracing ourselves
as the gunshots erupted around us.

I could feel the tension and stress mounting inside me. I glanced over at the van, which now seemed miles away from us. I knew there was no way we could make the twenty-yard sprint back to the vehicle without being shot. And if we stayed where we were, chances were good that we would all soon be dead.

My head felt like it was going to explode. These women were my responsibility and I had no idea how to protect them.

Almost instinctively, my hand brushed against the two-way radio I carried on my belt. Without thinking, I grabbed it, pushed the button and started talking.

"This is Friend One," I said calmly into the receiver, repeating the handle I used for the Lebanese AID operation. "Can anyone from IDF read me?"

Twenty seconds later a voice crackled over the two-way radio.

"Yes, we read you Friend One."

I could hear the general's voice in my mind, stressing that he couldn't spare security for me or my operation. I knew this wasn't going to go over well. But I couldn't think of anything else to do.

I took a deep breath to steady myself.

"I'm here at Beaufort Castle with a volunteer medical team," I said into the radio. "We have incoming fire. Can you assist?"

I could see the nurse and doctor holding onto each other as another bullet bounced off the rock in front of us. *We need your help Lord*, I pleaded in my mind. *Please guide us to safety.*

"Stand by, Friend One. Stand by," the voice crackled into the receiver.

Within a minute, two jets were roaring up the valley. Once again the voice came through the radio.

"Friend One, we have you in sight," the voice said. "Proceed to your vehicle, Friend One. Proceed to your vehicle. We have you covered."

The three of us sprinted to the safety of the van while the jets hovered overhead. It was so surreal it was hard to believe: the Israeli Defense Force had just rescued us.

I expected to get an earful from the general. I worried that he might pull my border-crossing pass or prevent me from issuing them to others. But no one said a word about my radio plea for help and the rescue mission that followed. Later I wondered if it was really the IDF that had come to our defense that night. Like that old fisherman who appeared to tell me about my biological family, I wondered if our rescuers could have been angels unaware.

Not long after that incident, I arrived in Metula to meet a new volunteer team and was surprised to find myself face-to-face with Salu Daka, the Rhodesian I had visited in the Mozambique prison seven years earlier. I hadn't seen or communicated with Salu since that time and he had no idea I was running the Lebanon Aid mission. Salu was now working in Switzerland with the Youth With a Mission organization and had come with a few volunteers to see what they could do to help.

"You look good, Salu," I said as I greeted him, knowing that no words could describe what either of us felt in that moment. "Looks like God had a lot more in store for both of us."

A couple of months into the relief operation, my son, Rob—now twenty—flew over to help me for a month. And not long after he left, Suzanne and Rheanne arrived for a few weeks.

Being with Rob and Rheanne made the long stretch away from home bearable. But it was painful being away from them. And though I made sure to travel home every two or three months for a visit, it hurt knowing that my absence and my work impacted my family both financially and emotionally.

I knew Ruth was pinching pennies at home, trying to make ends meet, and I recognized how difficult it was for the children to have me gone all the time. A picture that my youngest daughter, Rhonda, had drawn when she was six or seven said it all. It showed me walking off the steps of an airplane, and her following behind me, holding my briefcase.

My heart ached when I thought about the message that picture conveyed. And I felt like I was going to explode with pain when I contemplated all the things I wanted to provide for my family but couldn't because of the hand-to-mouth existence that came with running my ministry.

Rheanne had started spending her summers traveling with me as soon as she reached her teenage years, and I knew how much she missed me during the long school years at home. My kids were everything to me and it tore me up inside to know that I wasn't physically present when they needed me.

When I was at home, I worked hard to make it special for them. I would give them rides to and from school and try to make them laugh by doing goofy things, like balancing a cup of coffee on my head and acting like it was normal. Once, to surprise Rhonda at Christmas time, I climbed to the top of our roof with a ladder and pretended to be Santa Claus.

"Is there a little girl named Rhonda who lives here?" I called down the chimney, trying to disguise my voice so she didn't know it was me.

"Yes," she squealed, sticking her head into the fireplace so her voice could be heard. "I have a sister, Rheanne, who lives here too."

When I had a little extra money, I incorporated special af-ter-school visits to McDonald's to buy them treats, and once scraped together the money to take Rob to a steak dinner and a professional hockey game because I knew that hockey was his passion. But I also knew that none of my efforts made up for my continual absence.

The Lebanon Aid mission spanned for nearly ten months. Finally, in April 1983, the situation started to stabilize.

I was at our London base taking a short break when I received a surprise phone call from the Friends in the West office.

"Ray, I'm glad I tracked you down," my colleague said. "I just heard on the radio that Lida Vashchenko is on a flight from Moscow to Vienna! Is it true?"

Lida was one of the Siberian Seven I had sought help for when I visited Wolfgang Vogel in 1978, and had continued advocating for during the five years since.

While the Lebanon Aid mission had taken up most of my time during the past year, Friends in the West had continued to work on the release of imprisoned Christians around the world. And the Siberian Seven had remained at the top of our list.

The story of the Siberian Seven was a gripping one. It start-ed on June 27, 1978, when eight members of the Vashchenko and Chmykhalov families traveled to Moscow from Siberia for a meeting at the US Embassy. The families, both practicing Pentecostals, had written letters detailing the ongoing religious persecution they faced in hopes of obtaining refugee visas, and had been invited to the embassy to plead their case. But when they arrived, a Soviet guard blocked the entrance, saying that they didn't have written permission from Soviet authorities to enter.

The desperate families pushed past the guard and rushed through the embassy door. But sixteen-year-old John Vashchenko didn't make it. He was thrown to the ground and nearly choked to death before being carried away.

The two families huddled in the embassy, refusing to leave until they received word about the missing teenager. Two weeks later the call came from an older sister who had stayed behind, reporting that John had been severely beaten before he was returned home.

"If they can do that to a sixteen-year-old boy, what will they do to you?" she had prodded. "Don't leave the American embassy." Just then the phone call was cut off and the families, terrified of what would happen to them if they left, imprisoned themselves in the embassy.

As I did with Georgi Vins and Salu Daka, I had ordered thousands of prayer bracelets with the names of the Siberian Seven engraved on them and had distributed them to faithful Christians throughout the West. I had also helped organize a large freedom campaign for the two families in London, in which more than five thousand believers had signed their names and notes of encouragement on a 25-foot-long banner featuring the words, SIBERIAN SEVEN, WE CARE!

After the rally, I had driven from London to Moscow with a small delegation of believers—including Rheanne—to hand-deliver the banner to the families so they would know they hadn't been forgotten.

The Siberian Seven were moved by our gesture. But their ordeal had already dragged on for two years by this point and they were defiant and guarded.

Before we left we all held hands and sang *'Til We Meet Again.* And as we parted ways, I repeated the words I'd spoken to Salu Daka at the Mozambique prison several years earlier.

"We'll keep working on your behalf until you are out of here," I'd stressed. "We will not forget you."

I had kept my promise and had continued to push for their release—as did other organizations around the world. But nothing seemed to help.

In late December 1981, Lida and her mother went on a hunger strike out of desperation, and by early February 1982, Lida's health had deteriorated so much that I had secured permission to bring in Ruth's cousin—a Canadian doctor—to check on her. That led to getting her transferred to a hospital in Moscow.

On our way back to Canada, we appeared on *Good Morning America* to share the plight of Lida and the rest of the Siberian Seven. A few days later I received a call from a friend in Congress, asking if I could come to Washington D.C. for a meeting.

"I have a message from Wolfgang Vogel," he said when I arrived on Capitol Hill. "He wanted me to tell you that now is the time for the Siberian Seven and he's attending to it."

I had great respect for the East Berlin attorney and had left Washington convinced that their release was imminent. But another year had stretched on with no end in sight.

I hung up the phone with my Friends in the West colleague and immediately reached out to my underground contacts in Russia, who confirmed that Lida had indeed been released and was on her way to Vienna.

My next call was to a travel agent, who helped me book a flight from London to the Austrian capital.

I connected with Lida as soon as I arrived in Vienna. There was a flurry of media attention around her. But once we were alone, she made her request.

"I want to go to Israel," she said. "Can you help me?"

Given that I was well established in Israel thanks to the Lebanon Aid mission, it was a fairly easy request. I managed to scrape together the funds to purchase her airline ticket to Tel Aviv and soon had her settled into a small apartment there.

I spent the next few weeks wrapping up the aid mission in Lebanon while we waited for news regarding the remaining six family members.

Two months after Lida's release, the word finally came.

Once again I found myself in Vienna, this time at the request of Lida—who had asked that I accompany her to the Austrian capital to greet them.

I was usually so consumed with the next problem that awaited me that I rarely stopped to reflect on what had been accomplished. But as I stood at the airport, watching journalists swarm around the two families, my mind traveled back to that conversation with Krista in Sweden all those years earlier that had led me to launch Friends in the West.

Keeping the organization going had been a continual struggle, with constant money stresses, continual time away from my family and never-ending political hurdles that kept progress at a snail's pace. But each time I considered calling it quits, the Lord gave me the strength and guidance I needed to keep moving forward.

As I listened to the seven family members share their story with the media, I thought about the letter I had recently received from a Friends in the West supporter.

"You know how you move a mountain, Ray?" the lady had written. "One shovelful at a time."

That analogy defined my ministry. By taking it one step, one shovelful at a time, Friends in the West had become the Little Engine that Could. One step at a time, we had managed to bring hope and healing to thousands of persecuted Christians and secure the release of numerous imprisoned believers. We had also been able to provide food and medical relief for more than 24,000 Muslim and Christian families living throughout Lebanon.

I didn't know what was next for Friends in the West. But I knew that there was plenty of work that God needed done. I also knew that if I had the faith and courage to keep following his guidance, mountains could indeed be moved—one shovelful, step, or person at a time.

10

Fall 1983

MY THOUGHTS LOCKED ON the friendships I'd made with the Shiite and Sunni Muslims in Lebanon as I drove to my monthly pastor's meeting in Vancouver.

From the minute I'd landed in the region, the people of Lebanon had welcomed me with open arms, inviting me into their homes and hearts during my yearlong stay. They didn't view me as an evangelical Christian. They saw me as a humanitarian who had come to help. And rather than view them as devout Muslims, I had seen them as mothers, fathers, grandparents and children who desperately needed assistance. Together, we had forged a team that had made a difference for tens of thousands of Muslim families.

Sharing Christian values through loving deeds rather than talk was the theme I planned to stress with the group of pastors who had invited me to discuss my experiences working with Muslims. But as I neared the chapel, the CBC radio news report caught my attention. It focused on the devastating famine that had gripped Northern Uganda and reported that an estimated hundred and fifty thousand children were starving.

My body clenched as I listened to the news report. After that first trip to Uganda in 1978 to meet with persecuted Christians, I had returned to the country with journalist Dan Wooding to capture their terrifying ordeal in the book *Uganda Holocaust*. I had fallen in love with the people of Uganda and knew I had to do whatever I could to help.

I began my talk by telling the pastors about the leap of faith I'd taken after hearing about the Israeli invasion of Lebanon, and about how the Muslim community had played a vital role in the Lebanon Aid mission. I told them about the friendships I'd made—and about my focus on spreading God's love through humanitarian relief. Then I shared the news report I had just heard about the famine raging throughout Northern Uganda.

"The situation there is devastating and it's similar to the situation I dealt with in Lebanon," I told the group of pastors, hearing the urgency in my voice as I spoke. "This is the kind of project that has a start and end date. You could sponsor a team to go into Uganda and do something right now to help those children. It's all about taking a leap of faith and taking action."

Two weeks later I was in Kampala, sitting in the office of the prime minister. I had met him during a previous visit and figured he was a good starting point. But when I told him about the radio news report I had heard and explained why I had come to the country, the prime minister stopped me.

"The German Red Cross is already working in Northern Uganda," he said. "Our biggest problem is in the Luwero Triangle about an hour outside of Kampala. That's where the civil war is concentrated right now and we have more orphans and needy children there than in Northern Uganda. Why don't you see what you can do to help them?"

I knew that civil war had broken out in the country after Idi
Amin fled and President Obote returned to power. But I had no idea
how dire the situation had become. The prime minister described a
bloodbath between the rebel fighters and government troops, with
rotting bodies covering the roads, widespread civilian massacres and
sick, starving orphaned children hiding in the fields—desperately
trying to walk their way to the relative safety of Kampala. The ongoing slaughter in the Luwero Triangle had become so bad it had been
dubbed the "Killing Fields"by United Press International.

"There are so many orphaned and suffering children and we
don't have the resources to care for them,"the prime minister continued, eyeing me intently. "We need help."

My heart hurt as I pictured thousands of children hiding in the
bush—hungry, sick and traumatized. I knew I needed to do everything I could to help them. As I started thinking about possible solutions, my mind jumped to the horrifying images coming out of Ethiopia. Like in Northern Uganda, Ethiopia had been gripped by an epic
famine and relief organizations such as World Vision were publishing
images of skeletal, emaciated children in an effort to raise money for
food and medicine.

It upset me every time I saw one of those images flash across my
TV screen. Those pictures were degrading and stripped away the
dignity of African children. Before I even realized it, I was voicing
my concerns about the images to the prime minister.

"I agree,"he said, "but they need to show those pictures to raise
money."

I could feel the heat surging through me as I shook my head.

"I don't think that's true,"I countered. "What the world needs
to see is the hope and potential of the African child. Right now they

send money to help emaciated children and they don't even know what's become of them."

I could see the prime minister nodding.

"So what do you recommend?"

I thought about the Ugandan children I'd met on previous trips to the country and how taken back I was by their joy and resilience. Despite suffering through unthinkable loss and hardships, these children remained positive and exuded hope. I remembered a young boy I had given a ride to while working on the book. He had spent the entire car ride singing. He had the most beautiful, jubilant voice—as did the children I heard singing during Sunday worship at Makerere Church.

"I'd probably start a children's choir and take them on tour so people could see firsthand just how much potential African children have," I said, still lost in my thoughts.

"Well, why don't you do it?"

I could hear the seriousness in the prime minister's voice and suddenly the absurdity of the idea I had just proposed hit me.

"I don't need to tell you that your country is in the middle of a civil war and famine," I said, unable to suppress the smile breaking open across my face. "How would I even secure passports and visas for the children?"

Those were just the first roadblocks that popped into my mind. It was all such a logistical and financial impossibility that I couldn't believe I was actually having the conversation.

If the prime minister understood the enormity of the challenges my idea posed, he didn't let on.

"I'll help you with the passports," he said. "I'll leave the visas and the rest to you."

Once again I could feel that pull inside me. Though I had absolutely no idea how I was going to make it happen, a plan began formulating in my mind. I would form a choir comprised of orphaned and destitute children and take them on tour to churches throughout Canada. It would be a fundraising tour that showed the beauty and potential of African children, with the proceeds going towards a children's home where the returning choir children could live and receive an education. And if we managed to bring in additional funds, I would use it to care for more children.

"Okay," I said, returning the prime minister's gaze. "I'll do it."

Even Suzanne thought I had taken leave of my senses when I told her about my plan.

"Where would we even begin?" she asked as we strolled through a Vancouver park with Rod Forest, who had recently joined our volunteer staff. "How would we possibly accomplish that? Along with all the logistics and red tape, it would be so expensive to bring a group of children over and care for them. We're struggling to cover our overhead as it is."

Suzanne was echoing what others had expressed when I told them of the idea. As devoted as she was to our work, she was also logical and I could hear the exasperation in her voice when she talked. From a practical standpoint, I knew she was right. What I was envisioning was a near impossible feat and one that I had been turning over in my mind ever since my meeting with the prime minister. I had started preparing a mental to-do list and it was so overwhelming it was hard to process.

We had to find volunteers willing to travel to a dangerous war zone to help us identify, audition and train a group of destitute African children to perform as a choir. We had to get permission from guardians to let the children leave the country and then had to secure passports and visas for them. Once that was accomplished, we had to come up with the money to fly them all to Canada, and then find places for them to stay while we booked concerts and figured out a tour schedule.

And that was just the start of it.

On the surface, it appeared undoable. But I knew with every part of my being that showing the world the potential and beauty of these children was the right thing to do.

"I realize this isn't going to be easy," I acknowledged to Suzanne and Rod. "But I know God is guiding us. And I know he'll help us succeed if we take the first step."

There was so much work to do that it was hard to know where to begin. But as a starting point, I reached out to Pastor Kirk Duncan, who presided over Glad Tidings, a large church in Vancouver. Glad Tidings had a strong relationship with the Full Gospel churches in Uganda and previously sent over missionaries to fellowship with the Ugandan Christians. It was through a member of that congregation that I had first learned of Idi Amin's persecution of Ugandan believers.

Pastor Duncan immediately embraced my idea for the choir and invited me to speak to his congregation. After the meeting, I was approached by Cindy Kilburn, a young woman in her early twenties who had a background in music.

"If you need help, I'd like to go to Uganda to select the choir and get them ready to go," she offered.

Dorothy Williams, a long-time missionary in Uganda who had been expelled during Idi Amin's reign, also stepped forward, offering to do what she could to help kick start the project.

Within a month, I was on my way back to Uganda with Cindy, Dorothy and Cindy's mother, Mary. Our plan was fairly basic: Dorothy would make the introductions with church leaders to get the ball rolling. Mary would help get Cindy settled and then return to Canada. Cindy would manage the choir selection and documentation process, and Suzanne and Rod would start working on logistics in Vancouver. I would work between Uganda and Canada to ensure that progress was being made on all fronts.

It was all coming together. The only problem was that I didn't have the funding to get all the way to Africa. My ticket went as far as London, where the others had a layover before continuing on to Uganda. I didn't want my new volunteers knowing just how precarious Friends in the West finances were. And I certainly didn't want them covering the cost of my plane ticket. So I told them I had an important meeting I had to attend in London.

"I'll be on a flight tomorrow and will catch up with you all then," I assured them as we parted ways.

I offered a silent prayer and then made my way to the Kenyan Airlines office, where I asked to speak to the manager.

"I'm starting an African children's choir and will be bringing children out of Uganda to do a fundraising tour in the West," I explained. "I'm going to be bringing your airline a lot of business and I'm just wondering if you could help me out by giving me a fifty percent discount on my airfare."

Within an hour, I had a ticket and was on my way.

I was used to third-world living conditions. But I felt for Cindy as we stepped into the small missionary residence in Kampala that Glad

Tidings owned and had offered to let us use. While the small flat contained a bathroom, there was no running water for the sink and toilet. There was also no kitchen in the dwelling. And though we had a hot plate to warm up food, electricity was so spotty we couldn't count on it.

"Are you ready to make this your home for a while?" I asked Cindy as we settled into our new living quarters.

Our first task was to head to Kenya to purchase a used car so we had something in which to get around. But even with a car, it was slow going. The roads throughout Uganda were so full of potholes that some were undriveable, and gas was nearly impossible to find. But we had a mission to accomplish and were determined to succeed.

Dorothy started laying the groundwork by introducing us to pastors throughout the city and surrounding villages. On Sundays, Cindy, Dorothy and I would meet with the pastors, get to know the congregations and share our vision for the choir.

"I promise that your children will be well cared for," I repeated to pastors and community members. "They will see the world, receive a quality education and will be as loved and provided for as if they were my own children. And once they are back in Uganda, I will make sure they are cared for all the way through secondary school."

It took a couple of months for the choir idea to fully take hold. But thanks to the relationships I had developed during my previous visits to the country and to the enormous respect they all shared for Dorothy, the church community embraced the vision.

With everything underway in Uganda, I headed back to Canada to start raising funds. I was so tired I was tempted to crawl in bed for a week. Instead, I headed to the makeshift office we had established in a dilapidated house owned by Glad Tidings and began calling every local pastor I knew to line up speaking engagements.

The pastors welcomed me into their churches, and their congregations all voiced support for the choir. Some believers even launched prayer campaigns on our behalf. But virtually no one donated money. It was the same everywhere I went. People cheered me on but were unable to provide the financial assistance necessary to make the choir a reality.

I could feel the pressure building inside of me. Weeks were turning into months but no matter how hard I tried, I couldn't drum up the necessary financial support to make a dent in our funding needs.

Cindy, in the meantime, was facing plenty of her own struggles. Everything was moving at a snail's pace. Because there were no phones, all communication had to be done in person or via word of mouth that was passed on to community members. And culturally, everyone operated on Africa time, which meant that people often showed up hours late to appointments or missed them altogether.

In the three months since I had been back in Canada, Cindy had held auditions and had selected thirty-one children ranging between five and twelve years of age for the choir. She had obtained all the necessary permissions from guardians and relatives, but now she was facing the monumental task of securing passports and visas for thirty-one destitute children. And she was being bombarded with hurdles.

"Some of the children are without birth certificates and their guardians only have a vague idea of when they were born," Cindy blurted into the payphone at Kampala International Hotel, one of the few phones in the city. "And on top of that, the man at the passport office refuses to give me the necessary paperwork so I can even begin applying for the passports. What should I do?"

I could feel Cindy's stress through the phone line. I knew that securing passports and visas for the children was going to be a challenge. But I also believed that the prime minister would hold true to his word and would help us get the passports expedited.

"I would go to the office of the Minster for Foreign Affairs and explain the situation," I advised Cindy. "Let him know that the prime minister is behind the choir program and promised to help us with the passports. As far as age and birth dates go, just do the best you can."

Between Cindy's persistence and a little government intervention, the passport forms were finally made available. Cindy spent days completing the paperwork, using a combination of guesswork and whatever information she had managed to gather from relatives. Eventually, the passports for all thirty-one children were miraculously issued. It took a few more months for Cindy to get through the visa applications, which included medical exams for each child to ensure they were healthy enough to travel. Finally, nearly a year into the process, the choir was ready to come to Canada.

But as hard as I had tried, I hadn't managed to raise the money to purchase their airline tickets. The small donations that had trickled in from my church appeals and a few small fundraisers Suzanne and Rod had orchestrated had covered the costs of the passports and visas. But now we needed to come up with nearly $20,000 for airfare. I was beyond frustrated. No matter how many doors I had knocked on, I had failed to do my part.

A familiar heaviness bore down on me as I headed to the Vancouver waterfront to walk and think.

Why was I always in this situation? Why was it always so hard to scrape to together the money to do what I knew was God's work? What was wrong with me that I couldn't get people to see the vision?

Anxiety gripped me as I racked my brain for a solution. I was out on a limb and couldn't fail. I had involved too many people and had made promises of a better life to all of those children and their guardians. I had asked them to trust me, and now I had to deliver.

"Lord, I need your help," I pleaded. "I've done everything I can think of to raise the money for the airfare. I don't know where else to turn."

I took a seat on a wooden bench and watched the waves crash into the rocky coastline. My thoughts drifted to my childhood and the happiness I felt whenever I managed to make it to the coast. I thought about my decision to immigrate to Canada and about those early days working in the travel agency business.

And that's when it hit me: I could ask a colleague in the travel agency industry for help.

I had recently run into Dorothy, an acquaintance I had made nearly twenty years earlier. She was now living in the Vancouver area and told me she owned a small travel agency just a few miles from where I lived.

I knew it was a long shot. But it was the only shot I had.

I rushed home, dialed the number to All Points Travel Agency and asked Dorothy if she could meet me for coffee. As soon as we sat down, I laid everything out on the table.

I told Dorothy about the CBC news report I had heard the year before, about my trip to Uganda to meet with the prime minister, about his request for help, and about the idea to put together a children's choir that would serve as ambassadors of hope while shining the world spotlight on the serious challenges facing African children.

Then I went for it.

"The children are finally ready to come. My only problem is that I have no money for their plane tickets," I said, hoping I didn't sound as desperate as I felt. "I know this is a huge ask. But if there is any way you could front me the tickets, I would reimburse you with the first proceeds from concerts."

I subconsciously held my breath as I waited for Dorothy's reply. I knew I was asking her to take a huge leap of faith with me. But I didn't know what else to do.

Dorothy was quiet for what seemed like hours. Then she looked at me and smiled.

"I know you are good for it," she said. "If you get me all of their information, I'll have the tickets ready for you by the end of the week."

∽

A group of supporters erupted into cheers as I stepped off the plane in Vancouver with Cindy, Robinah, and Rosette—volunteer chaperones from Uganda—and thirty-one beautiful Ugandan children.

It was September 1984, more than a year since I had heard the CBC news report that had led to this moment. It was such a surreal feeling it was hard to process.

We had done it.

Against all odds and with virtually no money or ground organization, we had managed to bring a group of destitute children out of an African war zone. God had heard our prayers and had shown once again that all things really were possible to those who believed.

Suzanne, Ruth and other instrumental volunteers rushed to hug the children and provide them each with a donated coat.

The children were starry eyed as they took in the energy of the airport—the sounds of the luggage collection belts, the lights of the departure and arrival boards, and the buzz of travelers rushing to their destinations.

Joy and pride swirled inside of me as I watched my family interact with the African children they had helped me bring over through the thousands of fundraising mailers they had faithfully stuffed into envelopes that they then licked, stamped and addressed while gathered around our kitchen table. I knew that they felt what I felt: that these children were now part of our family.

I introduced the African children to their host families from Glad Tidings and got them settled for the night before heading home to get some sleep. It wasn't until the following morning that worry began creeping back in. Yes, we had miraculously managed to get the children to Canada. But now they were in our care and the responsibility was daunting. I was the legal guardian to thirty-one children ages five through twelve—most of whom couldn't even speak English.

Many of them were malnourished and had come to Canada with only the clothes they were wearing. They had lived through unimaginable trauma and I didn't know what kind of toll it had taken on them emotionally. They had also all had their schooling interrupted by the war and many of them couldn't yet read or write.

In addition to ensuring they were cared for and loved, we had to make sure they all received a quality education. We also had to finish training them so they could begin to perform, and we needed to start lining up concerts as quickly as possible so we could repay the airfare tickets, cover ongoing expenses and raise money for the children's home in Uganda.

I convinced Paul Mickelson, a well-known Christian musician who had served as Billy Graham's organist, to come to Vancouver and help us put the first concert program together.

While he and Cindy worked with the children, Suzanne and I recruited Bob Carson from the Bible Fellowship church in Surrey to train our chaperones in the Christian-based curriculum he taught at the Bible Fellowship Christian School. Rhonda also got involved—

working with Suzanne to make colorful posters for the children to use as props during their concerts.

My days were so busy with the logistics of overseeing the children and getting the choir tour up and going, that I didn't have much time to think. But at night I would stare at my bedroom ceiling, my head spinning as I thought about the choir and the enormity of the project we had taken on.

As usual, my vision had focused on the end result. But this time I wondered if I had bitten off too much. I had expected that the children would generate so much excitement and media coverage that we would have no shortage of concert bookings once they arrived in Canada. But after a couple of small newspaper stories and initial concerts at Glad Tidings, Bible Fellowship and a few other churches in the greater Vancouver area, we had hit a wall.

The choir's arrival had coincided with the start of a large Billy Graham crusade in Vancouver, which was consuming nearly all of the Christian churches in the city. And whenever Rod contacted churches outside of Vancouver and explained that booking a concert included securing host families for thirty-one African children and several chaperones, they politely declined.

I could feel my panic closing in. I had expected to repay Dorothy within a month of the choir's arrival. But the month was coming to a close and we had nowhere near the money we needed.

Rod continued to pound away at the booking efforts while Suzanne, Cindy and a few other volunteers oversaw the children and ensured that they were receiving daily school instruction.

I spent my time working the phone and praying for a miracle.

It was early November when Rod secured an invitation for the children to perform at the weekly noon chapel at Trinity Western University.

I was happy that the college students would be able to experience the power of the choir. But from a fundraising perspective, I couldn't see what good it would do. These were college students and I knew they wouldn't have much money to donate.

There was a buzz of chatter as the students filed into the auditorium, but silence engulfed the venue as the lights dimmed and the children took the stage.

As usual, I started the program by telling the students about the famine and war raging throughout Uganda and about the horrific circumstances these children had endured. Then I talked about the resilience and beauty of African children and introduced the choir children as princes and princesses who had come to them as ambassadors of Hope. One by one, the children stepped forward and shared their names and ages in broken English.

Cheers and applause erupted after each child spoke. And by the time the singing and dancing started, there was so much energy in the auditorium I could feel it charging through me.

I could see tears in some of the students eyes as the children wrapped up their program with the song "He's Got the Whole World in His hands." For the first time since embarking on the choir idea, I didn't think about finances. Instead I thought about the main purpose of the mission: to show the world the beauty, dignity and unlimited potential of African children. This is what I had envisioned and hoped for—that these young African children could touch the hearts and souls of Western audiences and show them just how much they had to offer the world.

Two days later the first phone call came. It was from a pastor in Los Angeles asking us if he could book the African Children's Choir for his church. When Rod asked him how he had learned of the choir, his response was simple.

"My daughter saw them perform at college and told me I had to bring them to our church," he explained.

Within a few days, we had more than a dozen invitations from pastors at churches up and down the West coast. Like the first pastor, every one of them had heard about the choir from their children.

We learned that Trinity Western University offered deep discounts to the children of pastors in the United States and Canada, and that hundreds of students from California, Oregon and Washington attended the college.

There was no question in my mind that this was God's doing. I could feel the stress leaving my body. The African Children's Choir was catching fire and taking hold. I didn't know where it would lead. But I knew two things for certain: the world was indeed beginning to see the potential and beauty of the African children. And I was going to be able to repay Dorothy and keep my commitment to the children and their guardians.

11

Summer 1986

NASR'S REQUEST TRIGGERED THE frustration that had been mounting inside of me for months.

"Ray, we're having difficulties in Lebanon again," my friend's voice crackled over the phone line. "We have a desperate need for humanitarian aid. Can you help?"

It was the summer of 1986, more than two years into the Lebanon hostage crisis that included the abductions of Beirut AP Bureau Chief Terry Anderson, American University of Beirut Hospital Administrator David Jacobsen and numerous other Westerners. Their terrifying ordeal dominated the news, and anger towards the hostage takers was at an all-time high.

Nasr, a Lebanese businessman, had helped me purchase and distribute food during the Lebanon aid mission I had organized a few years earlier and had figured I could start it up again. But as much as I felt for the people of Lebanon, I knew my hands were tied.

"Nasr, there isn't a hope in Haiti that I can help you at this point," I said, feeling the fire surging through me as I spoke. "There is so much concern about the Western hostages that Lebanon isn't popular with anyone right now."

My mind replayed the desperate conversations I'd had with David Jacobsen's son, Eric, to whom I'd recently been introduced. The families of the hostages were suffering so much and I could only imagine the fear and despair of the hostages themselves. I had been so moved by their plight that earlier in the spring, I had ordered thousands of prayer bracelets engraved with each of the Western hostages' names and had begun pleading with Christian congregations and Friends in the West supporters to pray for their release.

Along with the prayer campaign, I knew that US, British and French government officials were aggressively pressing for the hostages' release. Yet nothing had changed.

"I'm sorry, Nasr," I said as I wrapped up our call. "I'd like to help but it's impossible given the current political environment.

hostages released,

uspected that the
—was behind the
power to do any-
again.
Nigeria, and have
now people who
know people."

Concerned about talking over the phone, I arranged to meet Nasr in Geneva a few days later to hear what he had to say. Without intending it, I was suddenly overseeing two very different missions.

After the initial slow start of the Choir program, it had taken off—with national television appearances and packed concerts throughout the US, Canada and the United Kingdom. It had been such a huge success that we were now on our second Choir tour, with returning Choir children being educated and cared for in Uganda with the concert proceeds.

I was thrilled that the Choir program was taking hold. But I knew God was guiding me to do what I could to help the hostages, and I realized that the friendships and trust I had developed during the Lebanon aid mission could be instrumental. So, while Suzanne headed up the Choir program and oversaw the growing number of volunteers stepping in to help as chaperones and teachers, I once again focused my attention on Lebanon.

Within a week of my meeting with Nasr, I was on my way to East Beirut. The plan we'd hashed out in Geneva was simple: Nasr would get me in front of "the right people." I would take it from there. I didn't know if I could accomplish anything. But I knew I had to walk through any door that opened to me.

Nasr began arranging dinners at bustling Lebanese restaurants, always inviting several connected Muslim businessmen to join us. It was up to me to initiate the conversations that I hoped could eventually get us somewhere.

The first critical step was discerning if the people I was talking with actually knew someone who might have direct information about the hostages.

It was a delicate dance, with both sides talking in coded language. I always started the conversations by telling them about Friends in the West and its mission to help imprisoned Christians and people in need throughout the world, and about the humanitarian aid mission I had overseen in Lebanon during the Israeli invasion. Then I would gradually steer the conversation to the hostage crisis.

"I'm leading a prayer campaign for the hostages," I would explain, eyeing them intently as I spoke. "I'm here in hopes that I can get people to join us in praying for the hostages' release."

It was a slow, tedious process. The Lebanese businessmen always talked in vague terms, occasionally dropping a hint during the course of a forty-five minute conversation that I would have to try to make sense of later. But on my third visit to East Beirut, I started talking to a business associate from Baalbek—an ancient city known for its Islamic fundamentalism.

"I'd like to do what I can to help you," the man said simply. "I know some people who might be able to be of assistance to us."

I'm not sure why I trusted the man. But it made sense to me that the hostages could be held by someone from Baalbek. At the very least, I figured someone from that area would know something.

My conversation with the man from Baalbek set the mission in motion. Over the next few months, we communicated via telex messages sent through Nasr. I was pushing for the release of all the hostages. But because I knew David Jacobsen's son, Eric, I focused my energies there.

"We are praying with David Jacobsen's family for his release," I repeated over and over again in my messages. "Please pray with us."

On the surface, I knew it sounded crazy to believe that I could actually make a difference in a hostage crisis that gripped the Western world. But I also knew with every part of my being that God was guiding me to keep pushing forward. So regardless of how impossible the situation seemed, I kept praying for the hostages' release and kept my dialogue going with the Lebanese contacts I had made.

In the last week of October 1986, after numerous interactions and several more trips to the region, the telex I had been praying for arrived.

"Your family friend will be coming out this weekend," the message read.

I could feel my heart pounding as I read and re-read the cryptic message.

I knew it meant one thing: David Jacobsen was about to be released.

I grabbed my phone and dialed Eric's number.

"Your dad is coming out this weekend," I told him, feeling joy wash over me as I listened to Eric erupt in cheers. "You should get on a plane to meet him."

I had already been looking forward to the upcoming weekend for months because my daughter, Rheanne, was getting married. I put the hostage situation out of my mind and spent Saturday, November 1st, celebrating the biggest day in my daughter's life to date. It was an emotional day mixed with joy, pride and a twinge of sadness as I thought about the daughter I loved so much moving away to start a new life with the man she loved.

It was after midnight by the time I returned home and once again shifted my thoughts to the telex message I had received a few days earlier. I climbed into bed and turned on the radio to the CBC news station. That's when I heard the announcement: David Jacobsen, the American hospital administrator who'd been taken hostage in West Beirut a year and a half earlier, was free.

The enormity of the news hadn't yet sunk in when I received the next telex a few days later. *"There was a choice as to which man was to be released—our man or another man,"* the telex read. *"Our people were asked who should be released. They said: this is the one we want."*

I was just an Irish-Canadian believer following God's guidance. But suddenly I found myself in the middle of one of the largest crises to hit the Western world.

Eleven weeks after David Jacobsen's release, Nasr connected me with the Lebanese businessman from Kano, Nigeria, who arranged the meetings with Sheik Fadlallah, the rumored head of Hezbollah.

And two days after I acted on my gut instinct and hand-delivered my letter to Lambeth Palace warning officials that Terry Waite, the hostage negotiator from the Church of England, was in danger, the news broke that he had been taken hostage.

Now officials at Lambeth Palace wanted to know what I knew. And within a few months, I was invited to Washington D.C. to meet with government officials who were also very keen on learning just who I was and who I had been talking with. That meeting had been triggered by David Jacobsen, who had told government officials that I was the person responsible for his release.

I told the government officials about my prayer campaign, my connections in Lebanon thanks to the humanitarian mission I had operated in the country a few years earlier, and my belief that God was guiding me to do what I could do to help the hostages.

I could tell by the way the government officials looked at me that they were convinced I was just following my faith and had no political agenda.

"Is it okay if I keep talking with my Lebanese contacts?" I asked the officials as our meeting wrapped up.

"We don't care if you go and we don't care if you don't go," one of the officials replied.

I continued my prayer campaign and my slow, tedious talks with my Lebanese contacts. Eventually they began dropping other hints of their involvement.

"Would an Indian with a green card be of interest to you?" one of my Lebanese contacts asked.

"Of course," I replied. "Every human life is precious."

A week later, a hostage of Indian descent who carried a green card was released.

During another trip to East Beirut, one of my contacts shared an intriguing piece of information. He told me that in an effort to prove to the US government officials that they were holding the hostages, associates he knew had arranged for a Coke can containing one of the hostage's fingerprints to be delivered to the US Embassy in Cyprus.

Though working completely on my own, I relayed whatever information I thought might be helpful to government officials, and when I told them about the Coke can story, I sensed by their reaction that I had divulged information only bonafides knew.

David Jacobsen continued to credit me with his release and as a result, I was also soon in talks with a highly respected counter-terrorism expert who had interviewed David. That man, in turn, put me in touch with the chief of security at the United Nations, who was also interested in what was happening with the hostages.

Months turned into years. I continued my tedious talks with my Lebanon contacts, continued the Friends in the West prayer campaign for the bracelets, and continued to grow the Choir program.

Because of the Lebanon aid mission I had launched in 1982 and the friendships I had established during that time, I developed a trust with my Lebanese contacts and eventually they began asking about remuneration, even though they still hadn't admitted any direct connection with the hostages.

"I'm just a believer praying for the hostages release and have no money," I told them repeatedly.

I knew it was a delicate balancing act and when they kept pushing, I came up with any idea that popped into my mind to keep the dialogue going.

"What if you were to write a book?" I proposed during one of our conversations. "I'm sure we could get a big publisher interested and you could get remunerated that way."

The idea took hold. Though I knew it wouldn't fly, I continued to encourage them to put their story on paper every time we communicated via telex, a payphone call or in person.

Months passed. Then one day I received a call from a Lebanese flight attendant who said she needed to meet me as soon as possible. I headed to a lobby of a London hotel, where a young, very nervous woman handed over a thick manila envelope she had been charged with. Inside were the opening pages of a manuscript that served as an introduction for the book. The words were explosive. They told of how beautiful Muslim women were used as "traps" to lure the eventual hostages.

I showed the book introduction to a friend, who in turn sent a copy to a literary agent so I could tell my contacts I had followed through on my commitment. I sent another duplicate to the Friends in the West office for our records. I kept the original in my briefcase and then flew home to Canada to MC a friend's wedding. When I headed to my car that evening, I discovered that it had been broken into and that my briefcase—which along with the book introduction contained my passport and other crucial travel documents—was gone.

I didn't ask the government officials I'd been talking with if the US government was behind it. But I could hear one of the official's words in my mind.

"You're not keeping a journal of any of this, are you?" he had recently asked. "If so, be careful."

∽

While I continued my talks with the Lebanese contacts, David Jacobsen was hitting the national news circuit, continuing his appeal for the release of the remaining hostages. He always made sure to show off our prayer bracelets and mention the Friends in the West prayer campaign—which in turn drove mass awareness for the hostages and huge demand for the bracelets. The Choir program was also continuing to flourish. We were now into our fourth Choir season, making me the legal guardian and "Daddy Ray" to more than a hundred and twenty African children. The concert proceeds enabled us to either build or lease several homes in Uganda, where we educated returning Choir children and made sure they were completely cared for. And with the money obtained from selling the England estate my sister Catherine had donated to the organization a couple of years earlier, we were able to purchase a beautiful Choir base in Arlington, Washington, where the children could stay and obtain schooling when not traveling. The facility, which included room for our administrative offices, was situated between Seattle and Vancouver—making it a great central meeting point for Suzanne, myself and Louise Short, who had started working more closely with the organization.

So many things were coming together in such miraculous ways that I knew God had taken charge of the situation. One such miracle was the high-level contacts I began developing in Iran.

It happened when an Iranian woman living in Vancouver approached me for advice on obtaining a visa for her husband so he could come to Canada.

As it turned out, her husband wasn't just any Iranian. He was a heart specialist and personal doctor to the Ayatollah Khomeini—who was widely believed to be pulling the strings in the hostage crisis. The woman introduced me to her brother, who also lived in Vancouver.

He, in turn, introduced me via phone to Haji, a friend in Iran who was well connected in Iranian government circles.

"I'll do what I can to help you, Mr. Ray," Haji offered when I told him about my prayer campaign for the hostages.

I didn't know then how the two Iranian men would come into play. I just continued pushing forward on all fronts, trusting that God was guiding me and would get me where I needed to go—even if it meant being closely monitored by government officials.

I didn't know whether the intelligence officials were from the US, the UK, or Canada, but I knew I was being watched. And after my briefcase disappeared, I was on a heightened sense of alert.

I first became aware that I was being followed in early 1988, when I was contacted by the Sheik's nephew who asked if we could meet for a talk in Damascus.

"The Sheik is going to Iran to meet with the Ayatollah and he wonders if there is a message for him," the telex read.

I knew the Sheik's nephew meant a message from the US government and I had none to deliver. But I decided to move forward with the meeting anyway to see what I might be able to find out.

As I sat in the lobby of the Sheraton hotel in Damascus conversing with the Sheik's nephew through his interpreter, I noticed a large Caucasian man sitting in a chair across from us. As soon as I looked over at him, he lifted the *Herald Tribune* he was holding and held it to his face—as though he was deeply engrossed in an article. There was something about him that made me uneasy and when I glanced over again, I discovered that the man had moved and was now seated in a chair directly behind us.

I could feel anxiety shooting through me.

"Let's head outside," I said quietly to the Sheik's nephew. "I could use some fresh air."

A year later I was on an overnight boat from Cyprus, headed to Lebanon via sea because the airport in West Beirut had become too dangerous for Westerners. I was officially on a mission to deliver a prayer petition containing the names of several thousand people who were all praying for the release of the hostages. But the real purpose for my trip was to continue talks with a top Hezbollah official.

I noticed that the tall, sharply dressed man who was sharing my cabin was studying me. I immediately sensed that he had followed me aboard the boat.

"Traveling into Beirut is very dangerous, don't you think?" he asked, striking up a conversation.

He spoke in an Oxford English accent and I suspected he was with British Intelligence. I could feel adrenaline rushing through me, but I concentrated on keeping my voice calm and composed.

"It's probably dangerous for you to travel there, too," I replied.

The man smiled.

"I live in Cairo and am just on my way to Lebanon to conduct business for the day," he said.

He was holding an issue of an American news magazine, and after a couple more minutes of conversation, he handed me the magazine.

"Take a look at this," he said, motioning to an article about the recent bombing of Pam Am flight 103 that had gone down in Lockerbie, Scotland.

My eyes scanned the story, which included headshots of some of the victims. I slowly took in the pictures, my heart sinking as I thought about all the lives that had been cut short and all the grieving families and friends left behind. Then I saw the picture of the man I would never forget: the man who had been eavesdropping on my conversation in the Sheraton hotel. The caption below his picture identified him as a top US government official who had been based in Damascus.

I stared at the picture a few seconds longer, forcing my face to remain neutral.

"It's just horrific," I said finally, handing the magazine back to the man.

He made small talk for a few more minutes and then excused himself from the cabin. When the boat arrived at the port and I reached down to grab my bags, I noticed that they were each marked with the kinds of small colored tags found in supermarkets.

Anger surged through me as I removed them from my luggage. I knew my mission had been compromised and that my meeting would have to be postponed.

I made my way to an outlying hotel and arranged for the prayer petition to be delivered another way. I left for London the following day, determined to keep my meeting secret. Twenty-four hours later I was on my way back to Lebanon to resume talks. This time, I made sure no one was following me.

Nearly six years after the launch of the Friends in the West prayer campaign, dozens of trips to Beirut to foster relationships, and hundreds of carefully worded messages and conversations; I received the news that tens of thousands of people throughout the West had been pray

es told me as

sooi   iother round

of t

: the hostage

crisis had started. Over the past year, numerous hostages had been released—trickling out one at a time. But several others remained in captivity with no release date in sight.

The Hezbollah leader I was meeting with didn't give me an explanation for why the hostage crisis was about to finally come to an end. But I knew from years of talks with my contacts in both Lebanon and Iran that the release of the remaining few hostages was contingent on one big condition that still had to be met. And I agreed to play the role of messenger.

In early December 1991, I found myself holed up in a London hotel with a cell phone and a landline. On one line, I was connected with my two Iranian contacts, who were strategically stationed on the border separating Kuwait from Iran. The wife of the anti-terrorism expert I had developed a relationship with was on the other phone line, waiting for me to deliver the go ahead news.

The clamps were squeezing my gut so tight I was struggling to breathe. I said a prayer in my mind as I waited for the message from my Iranian contacts, pleading with God to let everything go according to plan.

The backstory leading to this moment was a complicated one that started with the arrest and sentencing of the infamous Kuwait 17 bombers in early 1984.

The prisoners—made up of operatives from Hezbollah and the Iranian-backed Iraqi Shiite group Da'wahad—had carried out a series of coordinated bombings in Kuwait in December 1983. The bombings, which killed six people and wounded more than ninety others, had included attacks on the US and French embassies. The terrorists were arrested and convicted in March 1984. One of those convicted and sentenced to death was Hezbollah operative *Mustafa Badreddine*, both the cousin and brother-in-law of top Hezbollah leader *Imad Mughniyeh*. This sparked outrage within Hezbollah, and the abductions of CIA operative William Francis Buckley, Rev. Benjamin Weir and other Westerners throughout 1984 were believed to have been a direct response to the arrest and sentencing of Mustafa and the other Kuwait 17 bombers.

In August 1990, when Iraqi Dictator Saddam Hussein invaded Kuwait, the doors to the prison holding the Kuwait 17 had been opened. But, though the prisoners were free, many of them remained trapped at the Iranian embassy in Kuwait City because then-President George H. Bush had launched Operation Desert Storm and American troops swarmed the city.

By this time the Ayatollah had died and Iran wanted the hostage crisis to be over so it could improve relations with the United States. Many believed that this was what had led to the release of most of the hostages over the previous year. But Hezbollah was adamant that they wanted certain members of the Kuwait 17—who were still trapped in Kuwait—back in the safety of Iran.

I gripped both phone receivers, each second dragging on for hours as I waited for the news.

Finally, I heard Haji's muffled voice coming through the receiver.

"They have just crossed the Iranian border," he said.

I could feel my hand shaking as I held the receiver, taking in Haji's words. I inhaled and repeated the words to the anti-terrorism expert's wife.

"They have just crossed into Iran," I told her.

Her phone line went dead. I knew what was happening next. A call was being made to officials at the United Nations, telling them that the deal was done and that it was time to dispatch a special UN envoy to Damascus.

On December 4, 1991, news cameras from around the world flooded the Damascus tarmac as Giandomenico Picco, the United Nations special envoy credited with negotiating the hostages' release, greeted Terry Anderson, the longest held and last American hostage. His release had followed the release of American hostages Alann Steen and Joseph Cicippio, who had been freed over the previous two days.

I spent the next few hours on the phone, celebrating the news with numerous friends and colleagues—including several people from The Associated Press, who had become close friends during the long years we had all worked toward this day.

That night, before going to sleep, I knelt beside my bed and offered a thank you prayer to God.

After all these years, the hostage ordeal in Lebanon was finally over.

12

Fall 1991

I HAD SUPPRESSED SO MUCH of my childhood pain that I didn't realize how much hurt was bottled inside of me until it all started pouring out.

The trigger was the film, *Hear My Song*, the moving story of Irish tenor Josef Locke.

It was the fall of 1991 and I was on a flight from Vancouver to Nashville for a quick meeting before continuing on to London. We were now into our seventh Choir tour and between the logistics of managing a new group of Choir children, juggling our expanding education program in Uganda, continually pounding the pavement for funding, and caring for returning Choir children—all while continuing to push for the release of the remaining hostages—I was exhausted.

I settled back into my seat with a Diet Coke and headphones, excited for a few hours of downtime. As the in-flight movie played, I could feel myself being transported across time—back to my childhood in Coleraine, the poverty-filled streets of Killowen and the war raging around us. I felt a tug on my heart as I took in the rugged Irish landscape and thought about my friendships with Jackie Dinsmore and his brothers. I was in the midst of reminiscing about the small church we had started when the actor who played Josef Locke began singing the Irish ballad, *I'll Take You Home again, Kathleen.* Suddenly I was seated in the parlor with my adopted mother, Lavina Ross, watching the tears flood her eyes as the song played on the BBC radio news hour and she thought about Willie, who was missing in action.

I hadn't cried when I was told that the Rosses weren't my real family. I hadn't cried when the drill sergeant assaulted me in my barracks. I hadn't cried when my birth father tried to explain why he had given me away as a baby. I hadn't even cried when my birth mother rejected me after I had moved to London to track her down and reunite with her. But now it was as though a faucet had been turned on behind my eyes. All of the hurt and trauma I had buried deep inside me was being unearthed and, no matter how hard I tried, I couldn't hold it in.

I turned toward the window so the woman seated next to me couldn't see my tears. I was embarrassed and confused. I was a fifty-five year old man. What was wrong with me?

My tears continued in my hotel room that evening and kept coming during my flight to London. Four months later, I was still crying. Anything could trigger an emotional breakdown: a simple conversation, a song, a setting, or a memory.

Even the news that Terry Anderson, the Beirut AP bureau chief who had been held hostage for more than seven years, was finally being freed couldn't stop my tears from flowing.

"Ray, I think you're mourning the loss of someone," Peggy Say, Terry Anderson's sister, observed when I met up with her to celebrate the news of her brother's release.

It didn't take much reflecting to realize she was right. For years

I had managed to seal off that part of me that desperately ached to belong—to be loved and wanted. I had convinced myself that if I just blocked out the pain it would all go away. But now, after all these years, I was once again that lost little boy—grappling with the intense hurt I carried inside me.

Shortly after my encounter with the fisherman, I had decided to once again seek out my birth mother, Margaret Barnett.

I was at JFK airport in New York when I decided to make the call. I could feel my gut tighten as I dialed the phone number I'd researched that matched the address the old fisherman had provided me.

My Uncle Harry, the man who had confirmed my mother was alive and living in London all those years ago, answered the phone. He told me that Margaret was working at a nearby hospital. But when I called the number he had given me, I found myself talking to a woman named Martha.

"Oh, Margaret's not here right now," she said softly into the phone. "But I know who you are. Harry's my husband and he's told me about you.

"Harry and I have a son, Glen, who lives here in New Rochelle. You also have an Aunt Rae who lives in town."

I hung up the phone with her and didn't pursue it again

Until 1985, when I was once again passing through New York City on my way to London. I had a twelve-hour layover and called to say I was coming to visit.

Thirty-three years had passed since that crushing encounter in London and I needed closure. I also wanted to meet my family members and learn more about my identity.

Three hours later I was sitting in the living room of Aunt Rae's house with Martha, Glen and my mother, Margaret. She was at least seventy, but hadn't seemed to age much in the decades since I had last seen her. Though older, she was still slender and nicely dressed, with her brunette hair hanging to her shoulders.

"Hello Margaret," I said, catching her eyes as I spoke.

"Hello Raymond," she returned quietly.

There was no hug, kiss or even a handshake, and no mention of our encounter in London. She seemed void of emotion and showed no sense of remorse. She just sat quietly on the couch while Glenn, Martha and Aunt Rae welcomed me into their lives.

I had visited her a couple more times during the past decade and had even flown her to Vancouver to meet Ruth and the kids, but I felt mostly numb when we were together. She was cold and emotionless and while I knew that she had her own issues and pain to deal with, I had stopped caring.

It was when I thought of Lavina Ross that my heart felt like it was going to explode. I had so much guilt, sadness and longing swirling inside me it was hard to separate my emotions. But one thought continued to scream in my mind.

Why hadn't I figured out how to visit her more? Why hadn't I made a greater effort to stay in touch? Why had I chosen work that paid so little and didn't enable me to do more for her?

Though it wasn't intentional, I had made a psychological break from the Rosses once I moved to London as a sixteen-year-old boy. And by the time I left Northern Ireland to head to Bible college in Canada, I was on my own.

None of the Rosses came to my wedding. They couldn't afford it and even if money had been available, I'm not certain I could have convinced Lavina to get on a plane.

We couldn't call each other because she was too poor to have a phone and I didn't write letters because I was ashamed of my handwriting—or at least that was what I told myself.

Now, as I thought back, I wondered if there was more to it. I had recently been diagnosed with dyslexia and Attention Deficit Disorder, which explained my lifelong struggles with writing and academics, and my continued need to jump from one project to the next. But I also dealt with extreme highs and lows, and sometimes wondered if I might be bipolar. And then there was the way I handled my emotions—rarely showing them. Had I inherited that trait from my birth mother?

As a child, I had clung to Lavina's side and hated it when she left the house. I would have done anything in the world for her and I knew she knew it. Yet as an adult, we never hugged or actually said the words, 'I love you.' Our love for each other was clear; it just wasn't expressed in hugs or words.

Whenever I was in London for work, I made it a point to go to Coleraine to visit her.

Jimmy Ross had died and she was living in a small apartment in the same subsidized housing development we had moved into when I was twelve.

It was always a surprise when I showed up at her door because I had no way to tell her when I was coming.

My favorite part was watching her eyes light up when she answered my knock and saw me standing there.

"Hi Mummy," I would say, feeling the warmth and joy wash over me as I took in her silver hair and kind, weathered face.

"Well come in and sit down, Raymond," she would return, a huge smile breaking open across her face. "I'll put the teapot on."

Our routine was always the same. We would head to the parlor and sit across from each other next to the fireplace, drinking tea as we caught up. Mostly I listened as my mother talked about life in the neighborhood, my siblings and the regular challenges in life. She now looked to me for strength and answers, and during those sporadic visits, I became the family adviser. I could hear her voice in my mind as I thought back to those conversations.

"That wee girl of Netta's living across the street—they threw a bottle of boiling water on her at work and she's all scarred. What should we do, Raymond?"

The last time I had stopped by for a visit was three years earlier. But when the door swung open, I found myself staring at a stranger.

"Oh, I'm here to see my mother," I said, thinking she was a friend.

The woman looked at me and shook her head. "Son, your mother's been dead a good while," she replied. "But you sister lives across the street."

I was so stunned I couldn't speak. My mother was gone?

I crossed over to Netta's house and knocked on her door.

"Why didn't anyone tell me?" I asked, still trying to process the information.

I could see the sadness on Netta's face as she took in my shock.

"I'm sorry, Raymond, we would have, but we didn't know how to get a hold of you," she replied.

I could feel the guilt closing in on me as I thought back to a collect call I had received months before.

It was from an aunt who was visiting her daughter in Toronto.

"Your mother's not feeling well and is asking for you," she had told me after I accepted her collect call.

I didn't realize at the time that Lavina was dying. She had numerous health issues due to a lifetime of smoking and had been in the hospital for several operations. But she always rebounded and I figured this time would be the same. The heartbreaking truth was that even if I had known that she was terminally ill, there was no way I could get over there at that time.

I was so broke I was struggling to put food on the table. The only way I could afford to travel was for work.

"I just have no money to get there right now," I had told my aunt. "But I will get there as soon as I can."

"Yes, please try," she had replied.

I had assumed that a few months wouldn't make a difference. But when the work trip had finally materialized, I was too late.

Like always, I hid my emotions and said nothing to Netta about the enormity of the loss I was feeling. But inside, my heart was crumbling. Lavina Wilton Ross—the woman who had taken me in as a sickly, three and a half pound infant, nursed me to life, loved me fiercely and believed in me when my teachers had given up on me—was gone.

I spent the next few months crying on and off whenever I thought about my adopted mother. She had been the most generous, caring person I had ever encountered—dropping out of school at the age of ten to care for her seven younger siblings and father, and continuing to be the family matriarch her entire life. She was the glue, the person who everyone turned to for help or advice. And though she had lived in extreme poverty and never got to experience the pleasures of a vacation or dinner at a nice restaurant, she had always given everything she could to everyone around her.

Sometimes, as I lay awake at night, I would think about what I would say and do if I had one more chance to be with her. I knew I would wrap her into a tight hug and tell her how much I loved her and how grateful I was that she had taken me into her home and heart, and had raised me as one of her own. I would tell her that her belief in me kept me going during those long struggles at school, and that her generosity and love helped me to become the person I now was.

Though I felt like I had a hole inside me whenever I thought about Lavina Ross, I didn't realize that it was her loss that I was crying about until the summer of 1994, when British documentary filmmaker Desmond Wilcox decided to do a documentary on me called Daddy Ray. We traveled to Uganda to see the work with the African Children's Choir, and into African war zones so he could see the overwhelming needs of the children we were fighting for. We also traveled to Coleraine so he could get a sense of where it all started.

We walked through the streets of Killowen, visiting the churches and schools of my youth. Then we stopped in front of the old Ross house.

As I stood there, staring at the earliest place I called home, a swirl of memories played through my mind: The dream about the checkered telegram that delivered the news about Willie missing in action; me, sick in bed with double pneumonia, listening to the doctor tell my mother I wouldn't make it through the night; the rent man coming to the house, asking for payment and demanding to know where my mother was; the swan's egg I had proudly brought home for food. Each memory started and ended with my adopted mother.

Desmond Wilcox was watching me and must have seen the emotions flash across my face.

"Who is the most important person in your life?" he asked while his crew focused their cameras on me.

I didn't need even a second to think.

"My mother," I said firmly. "My mother, Lavina Ross."

13

Spring 1994

I DIDN'T KNOW WHY I had been summoned to meet with John
Garang, the leader of the Sudan People's Liberation Army.

But I could feel the tension in the air when I arrived at his
Nairobi office, and could see the stress on his face even before he
spoke.

"Ray, the battle isn't going well," the SPLA leader confided as
soon as we were alone. "We are being pushed across the border into
Uganda and are facing defeat. Is there anything you can do to help?"

Dr. John Garang, who had been educated in the US, was a sea-
soned fighter who had been battling the country's Islamic government and strict military rule for years. The Sudanese government,
headquartered in Khartoum in Northern Sudan, had declared a strict
form of Sharia Law that stripped women of their rights and called for
barbaric punishments, such as stoning adulterers to death. The Islamic extremists who controlled the government were intent on turning
Sudan into an Islamic state. They were also intent on controlling the
land in Southern Sudan, which was considered a goldmine because
of its rich, untapped oil reserves.

Government troops arrived in villages on horseback—burning

down everything in sight and torturing, raping and slaughtering residents. Girls were being kidnapped and turned into sex slaves; young boys were being forced to join the fighting or be killed. On top of it all, the country was gripped by an unrelenting famine that had already ravished neighboring Somalia—where I had spent several months coordinating food shipments thanks to an emergency Choir tour in Northern Ireland that had raised 100,000 pounds for the Somalia relief effort.

I had met with the SPLA leader before and had been struck by his steely determination and strength. But now I could hear desperation in his voice and knew the situation was dire.

John Garang's words slammed from one side of my brain to the other. I could hear them screaming in my mind and could feel my own desperation creeping through me as their meaning took hold.

I had been working in Southern Sudan for nine months—driven to the country both by the devastating famine that had taken over the region and the gut-wrenching story of the Lost Boys that I had read about in *Life* magazine. We'd been using the current Choir tour to shine the spotlight on Southern Sudan and raise money for food, medicine and school supplies. But, as usual, Friends in the West was operating on a shoestring budget and we were scrambling just to keep the small relief shipments coming. How did he expect me to help him fight the war?

The room was silent and I could feel John Garang's eyes on me, waiting for my reply.

My hands curled into fists and I could feel the familiar heat surging through me as I struggled to find the right words.

"John, I'd like to help you but I have absolutely no money," I said finally, forcing myself to meet his gaze. "I just don't know what I can do."

I left his office and started walking aimlessly through the streets of Nairobi, trying to process the information I had just been given and come up with a plan.

It had been such an intense nine months with so many crises to address it had been hard to know where to begin.

As a first step, I had secured an agreement with the United Nations that enabled Friends in the West to work under the protective flag of the UN. This made it possible for our volunteers to stay at the UN compound in Lokichogio, a Northern Kenya town situated near the Southern Sudan border, and deliver food and medical supplies to areas overseen by the international organization. I registered the US Friends in the West organization under the UN. But I kept the Canadian arm of Friends in the West independent—enabling us to work in other parts of the country without UN restrictions.

While the United Nations oversaw flights into a region known as the Death Triangle because of the convergence of government troops and the severity of the famine there, they had no presence in Kajo Keji, a region of Southern Sudan located near the border of Uganda. That's where Manase Lomole Waya, a humanitarian I had met a couple years earlier, was operating Humanitarian Assistance Southern Sudan (HASS), a small organization struggling to make a dent in the overwhelming needs.

I felt like I was battling a raging forest fire with buckets of water. Everywhere we went we encountered the same, desperate circumstances: skeletal, emaciated people battling starvation, malaria and other deadly diseases—while living with the terrifying knowledge that government troops could show up at any time and finish them off. Unlike Uganda, Southern Sudan had no infrastructure. It was vast bush country and desert, with temperatures soaring to 115 degrees. Yet when Suzanne and I made our first trip into the "Death

Triangle" to assess the situation, we saw women wearing nothing but heavy sweaters to cover their torsos and noticed one man dressed head to toe in a winter ski suit.

"It's all they have," one of the UN officials who had taken us into the area explained. "People donate clothes and they wear whatever is given to them."

While we accessed the UN-controlled areas by plane and immediately flew to safety whenever word came that government troops were closing in, our only way into Keji Kejo where Manase had his base, was by an old Land Rover that had a worn mattress tied to the ceiling of the vehicle.

This was crucial because the only roads in the area had been carved out by the British decades earlier, and were so full of deep ruts that we sometimes hit our head on the ceiling as we drove. The going was so slow that it took us several hours to travel the forty miles from a Northern Uganda outpost to the base. And that was during the dry season. When the rainy season hit, some sections were impassable by vehicle, forcing us to make part of the journey on foot.

While a few of our volunteers stayed at the UN base and delivered ongoing food and medical shipments to the UN-sanctioned areas, several others of us started working with Manase to re-establish the village and a sustainable way of life. Despite the ongoing civil war in the area, a team of us managed to bring in a grinding mill, enabling villagers to grind corn into Sorghum, their main food source. We also began establishing schools under trees, providing structure for children that included at least one meal a day for them.

"It's your job to go to school and get an education." I told the first group of children that Manase had helped assemble. "If you do that, I promise you I'll go back to the West and beg on my hands and knees, if necessary, to raise the money to get you the school supplies, food and clothing you need to succeed."

Through Manase, I was also able to locate the remainder of the Lost Boys. Their story was heartbreaking. Starting in 1987, an estimated 20,000 boys—many as young as six or seven—had fled their families and villages in Southern Sudan to escape the civil war and certain death or abduction into the government army. Over the next four years, they walked a thousand miles, wandering in and out of war zones as they desperately sought safety. Thousands of boys lost their lives to hunger, dehydration, and exhaustion. Some were attacked and killed by wild animals; others drowned crossing rivers, and many were caught in the crossfire of fighting forces. The boys first fled to Ethiopia. But war erupted there in 1991, sending them fleeing again. A year later, an estimated ten thousand boys ranging in age from eight to eighteen began trickling into Northern Kenya and Natinga, a mountainous region in Southern Sudan. Natinga is where I found them, living in a sprawling camp comprised of parched mud huts that they had constructed.

There were no schools in the camp and we immediately set to work, identifying older leaders who could serve as teachers, and establishing several makeshift schools. We then shipped in basic educational materials and school supplies so the boys could start learning to read and write.

"I'm going to share your story with the world," I promised a large group of boys who had gathered during our first trip into the camp. "I'm going to do everything I can to get you help."

Amid all the other projects we were facilitating, I turned my attention to another nightmare: the Nuba Mountains, where the vast majority of residents were Muslim. The area was under siege by government troops and I'd received horrific reports from a Nuba contact about people being systematically lined up and shot. The Nuba people were sick and starving, but it was too dangerous to make food drops in the area. The best I could do was charter a small plane and fly food and medical supplies into *Pariang*, a small outpost south of the Nuba Mountains. It took residents twenty-four hours to make the dangerous trek to Pariang to retrieve supplies. But they did it without fail and I was determined to keep doing whatever it took to help them.

Now I was being personally targeted, and worried that my work there was in jeopardy. Two weeks earlier, as we arrived for a regular food delivery, my pilot had narrowly missed a large, unexploded bomb that was sitting on our tiny dirt airstrip. I had taken pictures of the bomb. It featured Farsi markings, proving that Iran was arming the Sudanese government.

I was angry. I'd been flying into Pariang under the UN flag and was supposed to have protection. Yet, despite complaints to UN headquarters in Geneva, nothing had been done to secure the area.

As I continued to walk the Nairobi streets, contemplating the enormity of the nightmare facing the people of Southern Sudan and the challenges I had run up against, my thoughts once again jumped to John Garang's words. That's when the full weight of what he had told me sunk in. If the Sudan People's Liberation Army was pushed into defeat, all of the people Friends in the West had been working so hard to help would either starve to death, be slaughtered, or be pushed into overflowing refugee camps in Uganda.

By the time I had finished my walk and returned to the house we were renting as a base, I knew what I had to do: I was going to take my concerns to the US government.

I called a travel agent and used mileage points to book a red-eye flight to Washington D.C. that evening.

I spent most of the flight thinking about what I could say that could convince the US government to get involved. I knew that President Clinton had steered clear of Southern Sudan and had refused to back the SPLA because they had received some funding through Ethiopia, which was backed by the Soviets. But I needed him to understand just what was at stake.

I had knowledge that Osama Bid Laden, the head of al-Qaeda, had taken refuge in Sudan. There was also growing evidence that the al-Qaeda leader had launched numerous terrorist training camps in the country. Without the SPLA, there would be nothing standing in his way.

I could hear the warning from a priest who had narrowly escaped the Nuba Mountains a few weeks earlier; it was the same cautionary warning I'd heard from other Southern Sudanese.

"If there's a fire on our floor, it will soon reach your floor," the priest had said. "We're in this together. Even if the West doesn't care about helping us, they need to get involved to help themselves before it's too late."

As soon as I landed in Washington, I called one of the government officials I'd become friends with during the Lebanon hostage crisis and explained the situation.

"I need to talk with someone from National Security," I told him. "It's important. Can you help me?"

The next morning I headed to the White House gate as instructed and presented my passport to the guards. Within minutes, I was being ushered into an East Wing office by two government officials who told me the office once belonged to Oliver North.

"How can we help you?" one of them asked politely.

We immediately got down to business. I told them about my meeting with John Garang and his warning that the SPLA was headed for defeat. I told them about the dire situation facing the Nuba

Mountain people, and the food and medical aid I'd been delivering to Pariang. Then I told them about the unexploded bomb on the airstrip and handed them the picture of the bomb with the Farsi markings.

"Whatever you think about the SPLA, they are the only thing standing in the way of al-Qaeda and an Islamic State," I told them. "You don't have to worry about communism taking over Southern Sudan. It's a former British colony and the Sudanese people would never go for that. But if Islamic extremism takes over Sudan, it will provide a strong foothold in Africa and will quickly spread to other African countries."

The room was silent as the two officials—a man and a woman— studied the picture of the unexploded bomb and the unmistakable Farsi markings.

"Your visit is very timely because we've just received orders from the President to convene for a meeting on Southern Sudan this weekend," the male official said.

I thanked them for their time and headed back to the airport to return to Nairobi. I didn't know what good my trip would do. But at least I had warned them about the danger of the situation and had done everything in my power to help the people of Southern Sudan.

A few days later I was sitting in the food court of the Yaya Centre, a mall located near our Nairobi base. Whenever I was in Nairobi, I made it a daily ritual to walk to the mall each morning for eggs and toast. I had just finished eating and was settling in with a cup of coffee and a newspaper when a headline caught my eye.

Israeli weapons 'bound for rebels' in southern Sudan:
Arms may be destined for SPLA fight against Khartoum

I was so stunned I nearly choked on my coffee. I quickly scanned the article and could feel blood rushing through me as I read the words.

"It is unlikely that the United States would supply the SPLA directly," the article read, *"but sources in Washington said that knowing American hatred of Khartoum's fundamentalism, it is probable that Washington gave the green light to an ally in the region to supply the SPLA."*

I couldn't know then that this would be the turning point for the SPLA, and that after years of continued fighting, the SPLA would eventually obtain what they had fought so hard for: a peace treaty and eventual agreement that gave them the ability to operate as a separate government.

I wasn't sure if my trip to Washington had contributed to Israel supplying arms to the SPLA. But I knew that it was God who had guided me to make that emergency trip to share what I had learned and express my concerns.

Regardless of how it had come about, one thing was clear: God had intervened.

14

December 2003

I WAS ENJOYING A MORNING cup of coffee with Mike, a South African navy band commander I'd gotten to know during my visits to the country, when he pushed a copy of the *Cape Times* in front of me.

"Look at this," he said, motioning to a headline about the severe drought and AIDS crisis gripping the Northeast corner of South Africa. "Sounds like they could use your help."

My heart ached as I read the story. According to the article, the Nkomazi region located near the Mozambique border had the largest concentration of AIDS cases in the world. The story reported that forty percent of the population was infected with the deadly disease, and depicted a community so devastated by AIDS that they had stopped holding funerals. It talked about thousands of orphaned children scavenging for food and a safe place to sleep each night. It also talked about the severe lack of water brought on by a drought that seized the region.

Getting involved in the war on AIDS was the last thing on my mind when we set up a base near Cape Town in the fall of 2003. We had come to the country to establish a world-class high school that our returning Choir children could attend when they reached secondary school. I viewed South Africa as a perfect springboard country to expand into other parts of Africa, and had been drawn to the region for years. With Apartheid finally over, the timing had seemed right.

But now, as I took in the words from that newspaper story, I knew our organization was about to head into another war zone to see what we could do to help. Only this time, the enemy was AIDS.

Within a week, I was in Nkomazi meeting with Sally McKibbon, a woman from Ireland who had established Thembalethu—a small relief organization that hired local women as homecare workers to provide comfort and relief to the sick and dying.

"There is so much suffering and so many needs it's hard to prioritize,"Sally told me when I asked what I could do to help. "But one of the biggest immediate struggles is water."

As we toured the villages that could only be described as a barren dust bowl, the urgency of the situation became clear. Sally told me that a water truck came once a week to deliver fresh water. But she said the residents had no way to retrieve enough water to last them until the next delivery.

This was an easy fix and something I knew we could address.

I immediately placed a phone call to Suzanne. "We've got to order as many wheelbarrows and five-gallon water jugs as we can and get them up here as soon as possible," I told her. "We need to get them a way to carry water."

With the water issue being addressed, we were left with a much more daunting challenge: How to help the thousands of children who had lost their parents to AIDS and were now struggling to survive.

Suzanne had flown over to assess the situation with me and determine how best to proceed. As we made the rounds with the caregivers, we saw firsthand just what they were up against. Hundreds of adults were in different stages of dying, and the caregivers were doing whatever they could to ease their nausea and pain, and assure them that their children would be cared for after they were gone. But with so many adults dying, there weren't enough left to care for the thousands of children left behind. The kids were doing their best to scrounge for food and care for younger siblings, all while trying to hold onto their huts and protect themselves from thugs who preyed on them.

We met children like Nothanda, a determined eleven-year-old girl who had been left on her own to raise her eight- and five-year-old brothers. She lived in a one-room cement hut with a large crack in the wall—making it structurally unsound. But she was proud of her home and did her best to keep it tidy, care for her brothers and keep going. One day, a man followed her back to her hut and raped her while her two younger brothers watched.

"She's one of the lucky ones," the homecare worker told us, fighting back tears as she spoke. "She tested negative for HIV."

While still trying to reconcile Nothanda's circumstances with the word "lucky," we followed the relief worker to her next stop, where we found a beautiful teenage-girl sitting in the sweltering sun on what appeared to be a white plastic sheet. A toddler stood next to her, clinging to her shirt.

"That's one of our body bags," our guide managed, nodding to the white canvas. "She's waiting to die.

"Her son is HIV positive too," she added.

Suzanne and I were too upset to speak as we followed the care-giver to our next stop—a coffin-making factory where children as young as ten and eleven were busy hammering together wooden coffins. Along the way, we encountered boys who stuffed themselves with dead leaves to quash hunger pains, and met groups of malnourished children who stuck together in packs for safety—sleeping on the dirt floors of anyone who would take them in for the night.

It hurt so much to see their suffering it felt like the hammers were being pounded into me.

I looked at Suzanne and saw my heartbreak and pain reflected in her eyes.

"Let's get to work,"she said finally, breaking the silence.

With Sally McKibbon's help, we connected with the principal at a local school to identify the most destitute children. Then we flew in volunteers to set up music therapy day camps. We wanted to foster healing for as many of these children as possible, while providing them with food, structure and a safe place to spend their days.

Along with the camps, we organized food shipments and brought in our Choir team so we could kick off the Choir program there. We wanted an Nkomazi Choir that could shine the world spotlight on the desperate circumstances facing the children, and at the same time, raise funds to support our ongoing humanitarian work in the region.

Everything was going well. Then, in the fall of 2005, we hit a snag.

It started with a phone call from my niece, Sally.

"Ray, they won't let us take the children to Cape Town,"she said, her voice filled with frustration and worry. "They said that they belong to the South African government and that their guardians don't have the legal authority to let them leave the jurisdiction."

My sister's daughter, Sally—who had become an integral part of the organization and oversaw our Choir program from Africa—was in South Africa, preparing to take our Choir children from their villages in Nkomazi to our boarding school near Cape Town.

The children, who made up our first South African Choir, had just returned home from a year-long tour and had been visiting relatives in their villages before heading to school. Now we were being told that these twenty-five children, who we had committed to caring for and educating to adulthood, would have to stay in their villages. The ramifications were even bigger because we had a second group of Choir children being trained at our Cape Town-area base and we were now being blocked from taking them out on tour.

I was struggling to understand why South African authorities would want to stop our program and prevent us from helping the children. The first Choir tour had been a huge success. The children had performed for South African President Nelson Mandela, had sang back-up vocals for the legendary rock band, Queen, and had performed alongside Sting, Paul McCartney, Mariah Carey and other world-renowned musicians at the Live8 fundraising concert in London's Hyde Park. The tour had been a life-changing experience for the children, who had big dreams for their lives thanks to the on-going education and support we had promised them. Now there was a real possibility that it could all be taken away.

"I'll make some phone calls and get down there as soon as I can," I told Sally, feeling the anger and stress take hold as her words sunk in. "One way or another, we will get this resolved."

I spent the long plane ride contemplating the problem that awaited me and reflecting on the journey of our organization. Eleven years had passed since my emergency trip to Washington D.C. to express my concerns regarding the situation facing Southern Sudan. During that time, our project with Manase in Keji Kejo had taken hold. The fighting had subsided and we had helped build a thriving community complete with fifteen primary schools, two high schools, a teacher training college, a skills training center and a medical clinic.

While still laying the groundwork in Southern Sudan, we had

headed to Rwanda, where more than 800,000 people had been slaughtered in an ethnic genocide over a hundred-day period.

I had been in my share of war zones and had experienced plenty of unthinkable situations over the years. But I had never encountered horror on that scale. Blood stained the roads and the air was clogged with the stench of decaying bodies. Entire villages had been turned into ghost towns because all of the inhabitants had been murdered; many hacked to death with machetes.

Those who had managed to survive were so traumatized that we decided to start there. We teamed with Dr. Ken Craig, a psychiatrist from England, to develop a four-part pamphlet that focused on how to cope with Post Traumatic Stress Disorder, and then distributed them by the thousands throughout the country. We also partnered with the Gisimba Children's Home, an orphanage that was overwhelmed trying to care for children who had lost everything. Along with providing funding for food and basic supplies, we took a group of the children into our Choir family—ensuring they were cared for and received an education.

There were so many nightmares breaking open across Africa that it had felt like we were constantly hopping from one crisis to the next. Now, along with battling the devastation caused by the AIDS pandemic, we were facing a battle with social workers that questioned our motives.

I contacted an attorney for advice and arranged a meeting with the social workers who were blocking the children's departure as soon as I landed in South Africa. Despite my pleas, they were adamant that the children were better off staying in their villages with their social network. And because the grandparents and other relatives looking after the children didn't have official legal guardianship, they told us the children were wards of the government.

It was clear we were gearing up for a long, expensive legal fight. And as an organization, we were at a crossroads: We could give up and return the children back to their lives. Or we could figure out a way to keep going.

It wasn't an easy choice. Without having a Choir on tour, we had no way to raise money to care for and educate the children. But we had also made a commitment to the Choir children and we were all determined to keep our word.

"If we can't take the kids out, we will go to them," I announced to our demoralized team as we discussed our options. "We will find a way to make it work."

Despite our convictions, we could all feel the despair settling in. As usual, we were stretched thin trying to keep our schools and operations going throughout Uganda and Southern Sudan, and didn't have extra money to cover the costs in South Africa without incoming Choir donations. But like so many other times over the years when the road seemed to come to a dead end and the walls were closing in on us, God stepped in to help.

This time, the miracle came in the form of our high school academy and training facility near Cape Town.

When we had first made the decision to establish a base in South Africa three years earlier, I had come across a sprawling campus with several buildings and beautifully manicured lawns that had been put up for auction. Because the property had originally been funded by DeBeers, only non-profit organizations were allowed to bid on the property.

As soon as I saw it, I knew that I wanted it for our organization. From my perspective, the campus filled so many needs. It gave us a beautiful location to provide a world-class high school education for our Choir children from across Africa who were entering secondary school. It provided us room to house and train newly selected Choir children before taking them out on tour. It also provided us with the space we needed to hold music therapy camps for vulnerable children living in slums near Cape Town. Beyond all of this, I had visions for a leadership-training academy that would prepare some of our older Choir youth for careers in humanitarian work so they could continue our efforts throughout the world.

The property was slated to go to the highest bidder and I had received guidance from an attorney who advised that I make an offer for 1.1 million pounds.

It was an astronomical amount of money. But I knew in my heart that acquiring the property was the right thing for the organization and I was determined to figure out a way.

As I prayed and racked my brain for answers, an idea formed in my mind. I knew it was a long shot, but it was the only shot I had.

With only two days to go before the bids were due, I caught a red-eye flight to London and scheduled a meeting with Sir Peter Vardy, a wealthy businessman and avid supporter of the Choir.

I had developed a friendship with Peter Vardy over the years— even staying in his home on occasion. But I knew that what I was about to ask went well beyond the bounds of our relationship.

I caught a Thursday morning train from London to Northern England, where Sir Peter lived, and was in his office by 10 a.m.

"What can I do for you, Ray?" he asked as soon as I was seated.

I took a deep breath and then went for it.

"Peter, I need to borrow 1.1 million pounds today," I said. "And I need to borrow it interest free for two years."

If he suspected that I was coming to him for money, it was clear by the look on his face that he didn't anticipate that size of a number.

Before he could respond, I quickly told him about the property

I'd found in South Africa, about the stipulation that it could only be sold to a non-profit, and about the other organizations clamoring to purchase it.

"Tomorrow is the last day they are accepting bids," I told him. "If I can 't make an offer by then, we lose the property."

Sir Peter let my words hang in the air for a few minutes before speaking.

"What will you do if I can't say 'yes', "he finally asked.

Despite my desperation, I felt a sense of peace wash over me.

"I'll understand," I replied, eyeing him intently. "I'll go home and have best sleep I've had in a long time because I'll know I've exhausted everything I know to do.

"It takes a lot of courage to come to you for this," I added.

Sir Peter Vardy stared at me for another long minute. Then he chuckled and shook his head.

"You don't give a fellow much of a chance, do you?" he replied.

Within a few minutes, we had struck an agreement. While I had only asked for a two-year loan, Sir Peter offered me an interest-free, three-year loan in British pounds that he told me I could repay in South African currency.

I got on the phone to South Africa and placed the bid. Within a few days, the property was ours. The fact that our bid was chosen was a feat itself given that Friends in the West was new to South Africa and that all of the other organizations bidding for the property had a long-established presence in the country.

The campus had been a wonderful environment for our Choir children. But we were coming up on our loan repayment deadline and didn't have the money to repay Sir Peter. And since the first group of Choir children was being forced to stay in their villages and couldn't attend the school, we decided to put the property up for sale.

That's where the miracle came in. As it turned out, the property value had increased considerably during the time we had it, and unlike the owners before us, we weren't limited to selling the property to another nonprofit. As a result, we were able to sell it for a significant profit. Even after repaying the loan, we had plenty of money left over to continue operations in South Africa.

We began scouring the Nkomazi region and found a building that had been vandalized and fallen through the cracks in Komatiport, one of the local townships. That's where we housed and cared for the children who had been accepted into our South African Choir family.

Even with that, we had enough leftover money to purchase a facility an hour north of the Johannesburg airport that we converted into the new secondary boarding school for all of our other Choir children.

The legal battle dragged on for more than a year before we finally had the opportunity to present our case before a judge. She listened intently as our attorney detailed our work throughout Uganda, Kenya and Southern Sudan.

Then she said the words that opened the door.

"Do you have anyone who can vouch for you?" she asked, directing her question to me.

I could feel relief sweeping through me as I thought about the one person I knew would impress this judge.

"Well, there's *Janet Museveni*," I replied.

The judge looked at me in disbelief.

"The president's wife?" she asked, referring to the president of Uganda.

"Yes," I responded. "She has been a long -time supporter of ours."

I could tell from the judge's reaction that we had reached a turning point in the case. The legal process continued to drag on for several more months. But we finally received the news we had been waiting for.

I was in Vancouver when the phone call came from Helen, a teacher who was overseeing the education of the children in South Africa.

"We've won!" she exclaimed in excitement. "They have ruled in our favor!"

A sense of calm came over me as I took in Helen's words. It had been a long, costly fight for our organization; a struggle that had impacted us both financially and emotionally. But we had stood by the children and had fought for what we knew was right. And with God's help, we had won.

I didn't know where the South Africa program would go. But the needs in Nkomazi were as great as ever. And now that the road-block had been removed, there was only one thing to do: get the Nkomazi Choir children—our ambassadors of healing and hope—back out on tour.

Above: Ray in his early ministry days.

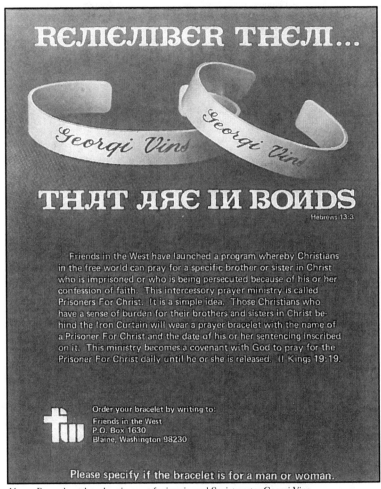

Above: Prayer bracelet advertisement for imprisoned Soviet pastor Georgi Vins.

Left: Guy Wiggins at his post in the United Nations in 1975.
Above: Guy Wiggins.
Below: Yanis Smits at the Congressional hearings in Washington D.C. in June 1976.

Congressional Record

United States of America

PROCEEDINGS AND DEBATES OF THE 94th CONGRESS, SECOND SESSION

Vol. 122   WASHINGTON, TUESDAY, MARCH 30, 1976   No. 46

House of Representatives

GEORGI VINS, SOVIET CHRISTIAN

The SPEAKER. Under a previous order of the House, the gentleman from Alabama (Mr. BUCHANAN) is recognized for 60 minutes.

Mr. BUCHANAN. Mr. Speaker, appeals have been pouring into the West in recent months from Soviet evangelical Christians, seeking relief from oppression by authorities in their country. Some of the appeals have been sent directly to the United Nations General Secretary, the World Council of Churches, the Baptist World Alliance, and Christian leaders in the West. Some are copies of appeals sent to Soviet authorities. In many cases, accompanying documents cite names, places, dates, and details of grievances.

A significant case is that of Soviet church leader Georgi Vins, 48, of Kiev in the Ukraine. Before his imprisonment early in 1975, he was secretary of the Council of Churches of Evangelical Christians and Baptists—CCECB—the dissident Baptist movement that the government says is illegal.

Georgi Vins, a founder of the CCECB, was arrested first in 1966 after a Baptist demonstration outside the Communist Party headquarters in Moscow and sentenced to 3 years at hard labor in a prison. He came out of prison in 1969 broken in health. A new case against him was started in 1970, but he went into hiding and carried on the direction of the CCECB underground. Late in March of 1974, the authorities found him and jailed him in Kiev pending trial.[1]

News reached the Western World in February 1975 that Mr. Vins was convicted by a court in Kiev of "harming the interests of Soviet citizens under a pretext of carrying out religious activity." The sentence of 5 years in prison to be followed by 5 years in exile was believed to be the maximum possible under the charge.[2]

The date of the trial in Kiev was kept secret, but family members and other believers showed up nevertheless and maintained a watch outside. The trial was held almost a year after Vins' arrest. Only persons with special passes, apparently those hostile to evangelical Christianity, were to be admitted to the courtroom. Several family members managed to get inside, however, among them Lydia Vins, Georgi's mother, who like her son and her husband had spent time previously in Soviet jails for her faith. She tape recorded her comments on the 5-day trial, and the correspondent of a religious publication in touch with key Soviet believers sent the magazine a translated transcript.[3]

Mrs. Vins said a Norwegian Christian lawyer, Alf Haerem, was obtained to be Georgi Vins's defense lawyer. Authorities tried to persuade the family and his friends to take an atheist as a defender, she said, but they refused. They, in turn, refused to give Mr. Haerem an entry visa, and Mrs. Vins informed the court of that fact. At this, according to his mother's account, Georgi announced he was rejecting the composition of the court.

The first reason,

He said, according to his mother's account,

is that the court is one-sided, consisting of atheists, and they are not judging me, but they are judging the confession of faith of the Evangelical Christian Baptists, they are judging the Bible and the Gospel, and they are judging the whole movement of our Christianity.

The second reason is that the entire investigation was conducted with much violence, with psychological and physical terrorism, and that the investigation was not conducted by the proper authority but by the Committee of Government Security (KGB). For two months an agent of the KGB threatened and menaced me, and now he is sitting here in this courtroom...."[4]

Soviet authorities also rejected the offer of the World Council of Churches in Geneva to send a foreign lawyer to represent him at the trial. They also rejected applications by other Western observers to attend the trial.

Mr. Vins's confrontation with the Soviet authorities resulted from his prominence in the Initiativniki, or Initiators, a group of reform Baptists who broke in September 1965 with the officially tolerated All-Union Council of Evangelical Christians and Baptists over the issue of submitting to the authority of the atheist Soviet state.[5]

The Initiativniki, which Mr. Vins served as secretary, have rejected Moscow's right to oversee their religious affairs, thereby prompting official repression.

The Initiativniki or Initiators, the "reformers," formed their own separate fellowship, the CCECB, now considered an outlaw organization in the eyes of Soviet officials.

In 1966, according to a report in Christianity Today, the AUCECB—the officially sanctioned religious organization composed of Baptists, Pentecostals, Mennonite and others—revised its constitution, apologized for the stringent 1960 regulations which prompted the start of the reform group, and asked the reformers to return. There was no effective response; at the time Vins and other leaders were in prison.[6]

One of those appealing on Vins's behalf through open letters to Soviet physicist Andrei Sakharov, who himself is in trouble with the government for his outspoken championship of human rights. In an interview published in a Stockholm daily before Vins' trial, Dr. Sakharov said Vins was charged with vagrancy—not holding a job and hiding from the police—using religion for crime against the rights of citizens—living on the means of others—and violating church-state separation laws.[7]

In theory, Soviet citizens enjoy religious freedom under article 124 of the Constitution:

No one is forced to be a believer or an atheist, to observe religious rites or not to do so.

Said Vladimir Kuroyedov, chairman of the State Council of Religious Affairs, in a recent Izvestia interview.[8]

In fact, religious worship in the Soviet Union is circumscribed with restrictions. The State Council of Religious Affairs is the watchdog successor to two organizations set up by Stalin to control "religious cults." Communist Party member—

[1] "Carrying the Cross in the U.S.S.R.," Christianity Today, December 20, 1974, p. 26.
[2] Ibid.
[3] "Soviet Imprisons a Baptist Leader," The New York Times, February 8, 1975.
[4] "The Trial of Georgi Vins," Christianity Today, April 25, 1975, p. 43.
[5] Ibid.
[6] The New York Times, op. cit.
[7] "Carrying the Cross in the U.S.S.R.," Christianity Today, op. cit.
[8] Ibid.
[9] "Soviet Subdues Religion, but Zeal for Atheism Lags," The New York Times, March 1, 1976.

Above: Congressional Record written by Ray Barnett and Guy Wiggins in March of 1976.

ship, the key to advancement in Soviet society, is barred to religious believers. Scientific atheism is taught as a part of social studies in Soviet schools and as a special required course at higher university level. But any religious instruction for youth is banned."

The New York Times this month reported:

The Russian Orthodox Church and the All-Union Council of Baptists function obediently under state scrutiny. But unapproved sects . . . have been harassed for refusing to submit on issues like conscientious objection to military service. Last month, the official press in Byelorussia reported prison sentences for several Jehovah's Witnesses found guilty of copying articles from the Western publication Watchtower and maintaining secret chapels.[1]

The case of Georgi Vins is by no means unique. Writings by Christian authors smuggled into the West tell of dozens of cases of repression of religious people. But Vins' case is notable and it is dramatic. His father and mother were imprisoned for their faith, and it appears now that his children may be because they have decided that they are never going to give up their beliefs.

Peter Yakovlevich Vins, Georgi's father, of German origin, came from Samara—now Kuibyshev. As a young man, he went to America for theological education not available in Russia, and spent his time there first at Western Memorial Baptist Church, Philadelphia, then at Colgate Divinity School, Rochester, N.Y., and from 1917–22 at the Southern Baptist Seminary at Louisville, Ky. On his return to the Soviet Union in the spring of 1922, he went to Siberia as a missionary. From that time on he was an active and wholehearted member of the Baptist Church in the Soviet Union.

He was first arrested in Moscow in 1930 after refusing the NKVD's suggestion that he support their candidates in the elections to the Assembly of the Union of Christians-Baptists. He was sentenced to 3 years in a labor camp, the first of several prison terms. His third arrest was in 1937, and there was no further news of him for many years. Then his wife learned he had been convicted by a closed court—the infamous troika—to 10 years in a labor camp without right of correspondence. He died on December 27, 1943, at the age of 45, in one of the Far East labor camps.[2]

Like his father, Georgi Vins, born in 1928, was an active member of the Baptist Church, and he also became a pastor. He received a higher education and holds two degrees, one in economics and one in engineering. He was actively involved from 1960–64 in the series of meetings and writing of documents to the State authorities, to the AUCECB and to believers throughout the Soviet Union.

Vins and other demonstrators were arrested when they openly walked into the offices of the Central Committee building in 1966. In November he and a co-defendant, Gennadii Kryuchkov, were tried and sentenced to 3 years in prison.

Vins and two other Baptists carried on an active Christian life of prayer and evangelism in the prison camp and aroused a great deal of interest among their fellow prisoners. He was transferred to another camp in an effort to stop this evangelism.

Vins' physical condition deteriorated in prison. He developed heart disease and had running sores on his arms and body. Despite his training as an electrical engineer, he was forced to drag logs at work.

Meanwhile, his family suffered because of his prisoner status. His wife, with a degree in foreign languages, was forced to take a job selling ice cream. His daughter was mistreated at school.

He was released in May 1969, and by the end of the year was once more taking an active part in the life of the CCECB.

Not long after Vins' activity as a pastor was curtailed once more. He was again arrested, sentenced to a year of forced labor—to be served at home—and 10 percent of his wages was deducted as a fine.

By June or July 1970, a new criminal case was being prepared. For more than 3 years, Vins lived in hiding, unable to return home and attempting to carry on his work as a pastor clandestinely. He appears not to have been arrested during this time, but in a list of prisoners put out in October 1970, he appears as "under investigation" presumably as a "parasite."

Vins wrote a letter in December 1970 to Russian officials to protest his mother's arrest on December 1, 1970. The letter contains information about prison sentences endured by other members of his family, including his father. His mother's cousin was arrested in 1936 and died in the camps. His uncle's wife was arrested in 1939 and spent 17 years in a prison camp. Her father was given a 5-year sentence in 1939.

The police came to Vins' mother's home on December 1, 1970, where her sudden arrest caused great distress to her grandchildren, who were in her care during the absence of her daughter-in-law.

The Council of Prisoners' Relatives—CPR—reported that her arrest was a direct result of her activity as president of the CPR in compiling and distributing information about Christian prisoners.

Vins' mother, Lidiya Vins, was tried in Kiev on February 8–9, 1971, and appealed without success on February 16. She was sentenced to 3 years' imprisonment. A CPR bulletin gave details about her poor health; she was diabetic, had a stomach illness, and had to be taken to work on people's arms.

Another CPR bulletin said there was no hope of her surviving her 3-year sentence because of her illness, and still another bulletin added that she had been moved to a civil hospital for a month, after which she was taken back to camp. Her friends in the Kiev congregation once more appealed for her release and she was released in November 1973. At the time, Georgi apparently was still hiding.

At the end of March 1974, Georgi Vins was arrested again and was held virtually incommunicado. The Kiev congregation appealed for his release to Soviet officials and his family pleaded to be granted the opportunity to see and talk with him, to learn about his condition.[3]

Only a little information about Vins' present condition has reached the West. Earlier this year, it was reported that after the January 1975 trial Vins was sent to the Yakutsk district in Siberia to serve the first part of his sentence—5 years of strict labor camp. The climatic conditions are very hard in that area, with the average temperature in January being 50 degrees Celsius below zero. Vins is in the category of "dangerous prisoner," which implies among other things that he has to report every third hour and that he may be shot without warning in case of desertion. Despite his poor health he is sent to hard labor 10 hours a day.

Left at home in Kiev were Vins' mother, his wife, Nadezhda, and five children. On September 18, 1975, the police confiscated most of the furniture in their apartment. The family was left with a table, a chair for each, and a bed for each. It is strictly forbidden for their church to organize relief work to help them.[4]

Mr. Speaker, a statement signed by Vins' four children asserts that Vins' wife was fired from her work in 1962 for her religious beliefs and II who years before someone would hire her. Daughter Natasha was fired in January 1975, from a hospital job allegedly because "religion and medicine are incompatible." Vins' son, Peter, has completed his education, but as of December 1974, had not been hired anywhere.

The statement from the Vins children, addressed to Soviet authorities, ends with a vow:

Our father is not released and if measures are taken in prison which threaten his life, then know you that our entire family is still alive to resolve to die alongside him. This we make known to you and believers around the world.[5]

Mr. Speaker, unless some action is taken on his behalf, Pastor Vins will surely die in a hard labor camp in Siberia.

---

[1] Ibid.
[2] Ibid.
[3] "The Vins Family," Radio Liberty Dispatch November 8, 1974.

[4] Radio Liberty Dispatch, ibid.
[5] Information made available by Friends in the West, a Basle, Washington organization whose President is Ray Barnett.
[6] "Carrying the Cross in the U.S.S.R.," op. cit.

Above: Congressional Record continued.

Above: Georgi Vins after release in April 1979.
Below: Gary Short, Dan Wooding, and others greeting Georgi Vins after his release.

Above: Ray in Lebanon running his Lebanon Aid mission in the summer of 1982.
Below: Ray in the Uganda killing fields during Idi Amin's reign of terror, early 1980s.

Above: The first African Children's Choir in the fall of 1984. **Below:** Suzanne Nelson in the former Soviet Union.

Freedom sought for hostages

by Valorie Lennox

Neither Islam nor Christianity condone kidnapping.

That, says Rev. Ray Barnett of Delta, was Sheikh Mohamad Fadlallah's response to his presentation of a 40,000 signature petition seeking the Islamic leader's aid in freeing 23 foreign hostages being held in Lebanon.

Barnett, who operates his "Friends in the West" organization from an office at Surrey's Bible Fellowship Church, returned Wednesday after a three-day trip to Lebanon to deliver the petition.

He made the trip, he said, because he feared increasing tension in Lebanon was making the hostages' position more precarious and wanted to take some action towards resolving the situation.

Although he intended to make the trip without publicity, 30 minutes after he arrived in Lebanon the media learned of his mission. That, he said, made his efforts to deliver the petition to Fadlallah more difficult.

Contacts he had made in the past while working as a relief organizer in Lebanon in 1982 after the Israeli invasion and while working to free hostages in 1986 helped him reach Fadlallah.

"He said that neither Islam nor Christianity condone kidnapping and the hostages should go free," Barnett reported Thursday.

Responding to the petition asking for his help in freeing the hostages, Fadlallah stated, "I am stirred by this issue which is a humanitarian one, although it has been placed within a political framework. I have sought to close this file with all the means that I have and am still working on exerting pressure to find the humanitarian solution to this problem."

Fadlallah observed the issue is not just local but is part of complicated political issues extending beyond Lebanon.

"I feel with the families of the hostages and I am doing all I can to reach a happy ending. Despite my limited means in this respect I will invest all my energies in this direction," he promised.

There are 25 hostages being held in Lebanon: Americans Terry Anderson, Thomas Sutherland, Joseph Cicippio, Frank Reed, Edward Tracy, Robert Polhill, Alann Steen, Jesse Turner, Lt. Col. William Higgins; British citizens Alec Collett, John McCarthy and Terry Waite; Frenchmen Marcel Fontaine, Marcel Carton, Michel Seurat, Jean-Paul Normandin, Roger Auque and Jean-Paul Kauffmann; Indian Mithileshwar Singh; Irishman Brian Keenan; Italian Alberto Molinari; South Korean Do Chae Sung and West Germans Rudolf Cordes and Alfred Schmidt.

Barnett hopes submission of the petition and of the petitions still being collected will help close the hostage incident.

Barnett also focused on the desperate plight of the Lebanese people.

"The hostage issue has in many ways obscured the fact that Lebanon is a nation held hostage by its own tragedy. There are thousands of orphans — Lebanon's children have known nothing but war.

"Hospital equipment is desperately needed to furnish more hospitals and clinics. Too many Lebanese people have died for lack of

Delta resident Rev. Ray Barnett points out Beirut on a map of Lebanon to his daughter Rhonda, a student at Bible Fellowship Academy in Surrey. Barnett returned Wednesday from a three-day trip to the strife-torn country, where he presented a 40,000-name petition seeking help for the 24 hostages being held by Islamic extremists. Valorie Lennox photo

such equipment," Barnett reported.

He urged individuals, organizations and governments in the west to help the Lebanese people, believing that such humanitarian aid will reduce the tension.

Barnett said he does not intend to use the publicity generated by this trip to Lebanon to promote another trip. However efforts to free the hostages will continue, with Barnett urging fellow Christians to form round-the-clock prayer chains for the hostages. Petitions are also still being collected.

The presentation of petitions and prayer chains are two of the methods used by Friends in the West to free those held in captivity. Believing in the power of prayer to effect change, the organization distributes prayer bracelets imprinted with the name of a prisoner, to a volunteer who undertakes to pray for that person.

Friends in the West has worked since 1972 to free people held in Russia, Mozambique and Lebanon. Another organization sparked by Barnett, Ambassadors of Aid, supports orphanages in Uganda.

Rev. Alex Palmer of the Bible Fellowship Church explained the name of the group, Friends in the West, came from the salutation used by Russian Christians when writing letters to fellow Christians in the west.

Palmer noted both organizations are supported by several Christian churches in addition to the Surrey church. Despite the publicity generated by the trip to Lebanon, Palmer stressed that the trip was not made to generate money for either group.

"This was not a fund-raising initiative," he remarked. "It was a fund-depleting initiative."

Above: Newspaper article about Ray's efforts to secure release of Lebanon hostages.

Above: Released hostage, David Jacobsen, joins the hostage release prayer campaign.
Below left: Longest held hostage and AP Middle East Bureau Chief, Terry Anderson, with members of the African Children's Choir. Below right: Terry Anderson.

 Associated Press

15 Feb 92

Dear Ray,

Just wanted to thank you, as much as thanks can express my
feelings, for all that you did during the past six years.
Madeleine and Peg and everyone else have told me about your
efforts. I'm only sorry I haven't had a chance to thank you in
person. Maybe that will come soon.
We're going to be on vacation in the Caribbean for the next
couple of months, then go back to Cyprus for a little to pack up.
Then we'll be in New York for a year, beginning about the first
of May, so I can write a book.
I'd like very much to hear from you, or have dinner with you
if you are passing through New York. Maddy also wants to ask you
about any children's homes or charities for Shia in West Beirut -
we'd like to do something from time to time.
If you have time, you can write us care of the AP in New York.
They're forwarding our mail. Mark it "personal" and we'll get it
fairly soon.

Sincerely,

Terry Anderson

P.S.
Maddy sends her love & gratitude.

50 Rockefeller Plaza, New York, NY 10020 212 621-1500

Above and following: Thank you letters from released hostages and their families.

7/9/86

Dear Mr. Barnett,

Please accept my deepest gratitude for what you're doing on behalf of the hostages.

You can't know how much it means to have so many people care about and work towards their freedom.

God bless you all.

Peggy Say
(Sister of hostage Terry Anderson)

*In my distress I called upon the
Lord. The Lord answered me and
set me free.* Psalm 117:5

*This is the day the Lord has made.
Let us be glad and rejoice in it.*
Psalm 117:24

Dear Raymond,

It is with heartfelt
feelings that we, the family of
Reverend Lawrence Martin Jenco, OSM,
say

Thank You.

The hostage crisis continues. The families
are in great need of your prayers and mine.
I hope one day to meet you.
With love —
Celestine M. Jenco —

Above and below: Bright Star Academy, a teacher training college and primary school built by Friends in the West during the civil war in southern Sudan in the mid-1990s.

Above: AIDS orphans in the Nkomazi region in South Africa in 2004.

My Identity

...

15

Early Spring 2011

" RAYMOND, I KNOW YOU'VE got questions about your family. Would you like to see some pictures?"

My cousin's words caught me off guard. It was early spring 2011, and I was in Coleraine for a quick visit after feeling compelled to make the trip from our base near London. Everything had gone wrong as I prepared to fly over to Northern Ireland for the day. I'd even misplaced my wallet. But I was so determined to visit my biological cousins that I'd made the trip anyway.

I'd gotten to know Annie and Marion over the years and often visited them when I was in the area. But we rarely discussed the past and no one had ever mentioned pictures.

Before I could respond, Marion who was now in her early eighties, headed to her bedroom. When she returned moments later, she was holding a worn 8 x 10 black and white photo.

"Raymond, this is your family," she said, laying it on the table in front of me. I scanned the people in the picture and immediately fixed my eyes on the one person I recognized: my grandfather. He was the barber down the street who always cut my hair when I was young, but never let on that I was anything more to him than a paying customer. I could feel the pain swirling inside me; feel the childhood wounds that had long been scabbed over but had never fully healed.

Annie and Marion pointed to the kids in the photograph and took turns naming them. There was their mother, Annie, the aunt I'd had the awkward tea with the day my biological father sat next to me on the bus as I traveled to my job on the coast. There was Maggie, the aunt who presented me with knitted socks whenever my foster dad, Jimmy, took me to her home for a visit. And there was Maude, the woman who sometimes gave me a six-pence when she ran into me at Sam Gouth's grocery shop. Annie pointed to Willie, an uncle, who was standing next to my aunts. Then she pointed to the baby, who was sitting on the lap of a man I presumed was my grandfather.

"That's Bob, your father," she said quietly.

I stared at the infant, a sharp pain shooting through me as scattered memories flashed through my mind. Suddenly I was no longer in that living room looking at an old photograph with my cousins. I was a young boy in Coleraine—aching to know the truth about my identity; aching to belong.

My thoughts jumped back to a summer day when I was thirteen. By now I knew that the Rosses were my foster family and that Bob Letson was my biological dad—though no one would discuss it or acknowledge it openly.

I was walking down the hill near my house when I saw Annie across the road. She was holding hands with a young girl who looked to be nine or ten. I'm not sure why, but I immediately knew that the girl was my sister.

My heart was beating so fast it felt like it was going to pound a hole through my chest. My legs trembled, but I forced them to keep moving forward.

I continued to glance across the street at Annie and the girl, wondering why no one had introduced us. Seeing them together was such a crushing blow it knocked the air out of me.

I kept walking until I was at the bottom of the hill and then turned back to look at them one more time. I stared at their backs, watching as the girl joyfully skipped up the hill as she clutched Annie's hand.

The familiar surge of heat rushed through me. It was everything I could do to keep myself from screaming. *Why did SHE get to be the wanted one—the one that everyone cared about and swooned over? Why was I the dirty secret that no one would openly acknowledge?*

My thoughts fast-forwarded a few years. Now I was a heartbroken sixteen-year-old boy—trying to make a go of it in London after the devastating rejection by my biological mother, Margaret.

It was my growing friendship with Mary—a beautiful, red-haired girl from home—that made me whole again. She was a couple years older than me and was in London pursuing a degree in nursing. I had first met Mary as an eleven-year-old boy, when my foster mom, Lavina Ross, took me to visit her mother—who was Lavina's cousin. After that, I would occasionally run into Mary at the local roller rink. Even then I had a crush on her and would skate up behind her and tug at her fiery red ponytails.

The one small problem was that Lavina Rosses' cousin also happened to be Bob's sister, my Aunt Annie.

I knew deep down that this made Mary my first cousin. But she didn't know. And since my identity was the dirty secret that no one acknowledged, I buried the information deep inside me and didn't acknowledge it either.

Mary and I started meeting for coffee and taking long walks throughout the city. At first I acted as her advisor, counseling her on her relationship with a boy that her parents vehemently opposed.

We also talked about our faith and I helped her find her way to God.

Her relationship with the boy soon ended and we began developing feelings for each other. One day, a few months into our deepening friendship, Mary sprung a surprise on me.

"My uncle, Bob, lives in the countryside and I'm heading out there for the weekend,"she said. "Would you like to go with me?"

I was soaring. Of course I wanted to go; it meant spending concentrated time with Mary. The fact that her uncle also happened to be my biological dad was an annoyance I didn't want to think about. We hadn't spoken since that awkward bus ride a few years earlier and as far as I was concerned, he was nothing more to me than Mary's uncle.

I spent the train ride relishing my alone time with Mary. Bob met us at the train station and, like me, pretended I was nothing more than Mary's guest.

It was a fun two days. Bob was living in a home with a woman and her two daughters. He said he was renting a room from her, but I suspected they were in a relationship. They seemed happy and I didn't think about it one way or another. I was so consumed with Mary that I didn't pay much attention to anyone or anything else around me.

The weekend was a blur. We enjoyed dinner with Bob and his lady friend and explored the town together. With Mary as my buffer, I didn't feel awkward around Bob. I enjoyed his sense of humor and the light dinner conversations we had.

It wasn't until a few months later that the full ramifications of that weekend visit became clear. Mary and I had both given up on London by this time and had returned home to Northern Ireland— where we continued to spend time together every chance we got.

Sometimes Annie and Marion—Mary's older sisters—would

cover for us by inviting Mary to babysit at their houses, where I could meet up with her. Other times we would meet at the beach for a walk. I knew her parents didn't approve because we had to hide our relationship from them and one day, while taking a walk along the coast, it came to a head.

"Look Raymond," Mary started, "my mother has told me that I have to break it off with you because she said we are cousins and it's not the best thing for either one of us."

It was as though she had just upended a wasp's nest. Her words swarmed around me, stinging every part of my body. I was in so much pain I felt like I was on fire.

"So it's over?" I managed.

"Yes," she said softly. "We'll keep up our friendship, but we shouldn't hang out every spare minute we have."

Though I was never able to confirm it, I suspected that Bob had played a role in our breakup. I imagined that he had written a letter to Mary's parents, warning them of our blossoming relationship.

As I walked the beach with Mary, absorbing the finality of her words, I felt another small part of myself dying. Neither Bob nor Annie acknowledged me as their own. Their rejection hurt so much it was hard to process. Now, on top it all, they were interfering in a relationship that meant everything to me.

My thoughts returned to the living room with Mary's sisters—my cousins Marion and Annie. Mary had since died and being with her sisters made me feel like I still had a connection with her. Sometime during my time travel, Marion had retrieved another photograph and was now pushing it toward me.

"Here's a picture of your dad as a teenager," she explained. "It was taken shortly after your grandmother died."

I glanced at the picture and could hear my breath catch. Bob looked to be fourteen or fifteen and was standing by his mother's grave. The resemblance was so uncanny that, if I didn't know better, I would have sworn I was looking at a picture of myself.

I stared at the picture of my dad, imagining the pain he was experiencing the day that photo was taken. For the first time in my life, I wondered what he had been like as a boy—what his passions and interests were; what he had dreamed of for his life. I had received a couple of letters from him over the years, in which he wrote about finding solace in the music at a local Pentecostal church he sometimes attended. But aside from that, and the fact that he had a daughter he had never spoken about to me and that I had never officially met, I knew virtually nothing about him.

My thoughts once again drifted back across time. I was in London again, only now I was in my late twenties and had a four-year-old son of my own.

I had traveled to London to oversee the Full Gospel Businessmen's Airlift Convention that I had helped organize, and Ruth and Robbie had accompanied me. The Hilton Hotel where the convention was being held had a huge fountain that Robbie loved and as I watched him play in the water one morning, I started thinking about Bob.

I hadn't seen him since that visit with Mary more than a decade earlier, but I knew he was still living in the English countryside and I suddenly felt an urge to see him. I tracked down his phone number in the hotel phone directory and slowly dialed the numbers.

I felt at peace as I listened to the phone ring. The usual anxiety was gone; I was in control.

"I'm here in London for business," I said in a matter-of-fact tone as soon as Bob answered the phone. "I'm here with my wife, Ruth, and our son, Robbie, and I'd like you to meet them."

We arranged to meet for lunch in the hotel restaurant. As soon as I saw him, I knew the tables had been turned. While I was completely comfortable with the visit, I could feel his uneasiness as he made his way toward me.

Though he couldn't have been more than fifty, my father looked old and feeble. I knew he had lung problems and had been in and out of the hospital. But I didn't expect him to look so sick.

"Hello Raymond," he said when he saw me.

"Hi Bob," I replied. "It's good to see you."

At first I felt nothing. But as I took in my biological father, I could feel the sadness seeping in. Only I wasn't sad for me; I was sad for him.

I knew that Bob had saved my life as a baby by taking me to Lavina Ross. And for that, I would always be grateful. But because of the secrecy surrounding my identity, he had missed out on his only son's life—and I could see that it hurt him now.

Our lunch conversation was awkward and forced. I told him about my work and asked him about his life, but in reality we were strangers and had little to say to each other.

Bob didn't eat much of his lunch. I wasn't sure if it was due to nerves or his health. Afterward, I introduced him to Ruth and Robbie. Then he, Robbie and I headed across the road to Hyde Park for a walk.

Three hours later our visit was over and Bob was back on a train headed to the safety and comfort of his home in the countryside. That was the last time I saw him. A few years later I received word that he had died. It was after-the-fact and no one had bothered to invite me to his funeral.

ᗌ

"These pictures are for you, Raymond."

Marion's voice snapped me back to the present. I was once again a seventy-four-year-old man visiting my two cousins in Coleraine. And after a lifetime of searching, I was finally getting the closure I needed.

I could feel their love as Marion handed me the two photographs and she and Annie enveloped me in a hug. I knew then that—like my Aunt Maggie and Aunt Maude who had found ways to do small things for me as a boy—my cousins, Annie and Marion had always cared about me; they had even tried to help me keep my relationship going with Mary. But because of the times and circumstances, they had all been prevented from publicly claiming me as their own.

In that moment, it hit me that in many ways, we were all victims of my biological mother. I could hear my father's words from that awkward bus ride more than sixty years earlier playing in my mind.

"I loved your mother and wanted to marry her," I could hear him saying. "But she didn't want to marry me."

I didn't know what my life would have been like had Margaret agreed to marry my father. But as I contemplated that possibility, I realized that had Margaret raised me, I would have missed out on having Lavina Ross for my mother. And despite our poverty and struggles, I wouldn't have traded that for anything.

I could feel the wounds beginning to close inside me as my hand closed over the photographs I'd been given. These pictures represented the missing puzzle pieces from my life—the pieces I had so desperately needed.

"Thank you," I said to both Annie and Marion as I headed toward the door. "You'll never know how much this means to me."

16

June 2012

THERE WAS SO MUCH electricity in the air I could feel it charging through me as I stood backstage, waiting for the perform...

Our Choir c... over the years an... including US Pres... never experienced...

A sea of peo... ace, all gathered... Queen Elizabeth'... casting the event... more viewers. An... in front of the pal... our Choir childre...

My entire b... mity of the mom... with Elton John, Paul McCartney, Annie Lenox and other world-renowned British musicians—all who had come together to pay tribute to the world's most famous Queen.

The opportunity to participate in the Queen's Diamond Jubilee concert had started with a phone call several months earlier from a BBC producer who was looking for an African choir to perform in a BBC documentary being made exclusively for the Diamond Jubilee celebrations. It focused on the Queen's sixty years of service and spotlighted the Commonwealth countries—which included Kenya.

Within a few weeks we were in Rift Valley, Kenya, with award-winning English singer-songwriter Gary Barlow and a BBC camera crew to record the children performing. It was an incredible honor to have the African Children's Choir included in the documentary. But from the moment the call came in, I was determined to figure out a way for them to perform live at the Diamond Jubilee.

It was the kind of request I knew I could only make in person, and getting that face-to-face moment was the entire reason I had flown to Kenya.

I waited patiently through the hours of filming for the opportunity to present itself. It came at the end, as the camera crew began breaking down their equipment.

I took a deep breath and headed toward Mr. Barlow.

"I'm Ray Barnett, founder of the African Children's Choir," I said, reaching out to shake his hand. "I just wanted to thank you for this opportunity."

The English megastar and recording producer acknowledged me and thanked me for making the Choir available.

That's when I went for it.

"By the way, I was just wondering. If we could get the children to England, would there be any chance they could perform in the Jubilee?"

"Absolutely."

Mr. Barlow's swift response caught me off guard. But now that I had an opening, I was determined to solidify the deal.

"Oh, that's just great," I replied. "Who do I have to talk to about next steps?"

Mr. Barlow smiled.

"You're talking to him," he said. "I'm overseeing the entire event."

It had been an exciting but stressful few months pulling it all together. We had a group of Choir children on tour, but they were already booked in concerts throughout the US. Instead, we pulled together children from recent Uganda and Kenya choirs and began training them to perform the song "Sing," which Gary Barlow and Andrew Lloyd Weber had composed specifically for the Diamond Jubilee celebrations.

The African Children's Choir was singing alongside the UK's renowned Military Wives Choir and other musicians from around the world. But it was one of our Choir children, twelve-year-old Lydia, who was chosen to sing the opening verses of the song that would enjoy only one public performance.

There were no words to describe the pride swelling inside me as I stood at the side of the stage, waiting for Lydia to start the song the entire world was waiting to hear. But the one thought replaying in my mind was a sentence I had often used to introduce our Choir children at concerts.

"These children are royalty," I would start out. "You are looking at princes and princesses."

I had known that the African Children's Choir would move audiences and change lives before we ever brought the first group of children out of Uganda in 1984. It's what I had repeated to congregations at every church I visited in an effort to raise money to make the African Children's Choir a reality. But even I hadn't envisioned how far the Choir program would come or just how big of an impact the children would make.

My original goal was to show the world the beauty and potential of African children and raise funds that would enable us to provide an ongoing education for the children accepted into the Choir program and care for them as one of our own through adulthood. But the children had exceeded that goal during their very first Choir tour. Now, nearly thirty years later, the African Children's Choir had grown into an international sensation that fostered healing and unity everywhere they went. Through music, dance and simple conversation, the children had been able to connect with audiences worldwide and shine the spotlight on the devastating circumstances facing children and communities throughout Africa. Along with caring for the children in our Choir family, the concerts had enabled us to raise funding to provide food, education and hope to tens of thousands of destitute African children, as well as emergency funding for one-off projects.

The Choir's universal appeal and power hit home for me during the Somalia famine crisis in early 1991. I had traveled into Somalia to assess the situation and had connected with an on-the-ground relief organization that was struggling to make a dent in the dire needs facing the people there. I knew we had to do whatever we could to help. And I immediately thought of the Choir.

I called Suzanne from our base outside of London and told her of my idea.

"I'm going to get the Choir over here and I need you and Louise to come as soon as possible to help with the logistics," I told her. "I want to get an emergency Choir tour going throughout Northern Ireland to raise money for Somalia. The people there are starving and we've got to do whatever we can to help them."

As soon as I hung up with Suzanne, I called Matthew Kalulu

to tell him of the plan. Matthew was the tour leader overseeing the current Choir tour and had recently returned the children to Kenya to be with their families for the holidays.

"How soon can you round up the children?" I asked. "We need to get them over to Northern Ireland as soon as possible. We need their help."

On the surface, I knew the idea sounded like so many of my ideas: impossible. We didn't have a single Choir concert scheduled in Northern Ireland. On top of that, we had no place to house the children during their time in the country, and no place to set up an administrative base during the Choir tour we hoped would materialize. But I knew in my heart it was the right thing to do. And given my friendships and roots in the country, I realized that if any group was going to help us, it was the church community in my homeland.

Suzanne and Louise arrived in London on a Thursday and immediately began composing a letter to church pastors that detailed the emergency concert tour we were launching to raise money for Somalia. While they worked on the messaging, I headed to a nearby technology store to purchase a cell phone—one of the first mobile phones available in the market.

Suzanne nearly flipped when she saw me return with it.

"What are you doing, Ray?" she asked, her voice steaming with frustration. "Those phones are expensive. We don't have the money for something like that."

It was the reaction I expected from Suzanne, who had managed to keep our organization afloat through tight budgeting. As it was, we were maxing out Friends in the West credit cards just to get the Choir children from Africa to Northern Ireland.

But I also knew the phone was essential.

"So how do you think the churches are going to reach us?" I returned. 'We don't even know where we will be in Northern Ireland. We have to include a phone number in the letter or they'll have no way to contact us.'

The issue resolved, we finished up the emergency appeal, added in the cell phone number and addressed and stamped dozens of letters that we stuck in the Friday mail. The following morning we caught a flight to Northern Ireland, still uncertain of what would come next. One way or another, I figured it would take a couple of days for the responses to start coming and since Suzanne had brought her niece along for the trip, we decided to take the morning off for sightseeing.

We rented a car and drove to Giants Causeway to check out the thousands of rock formations caused by an ancient volcano. I handed the cell phone to Louise and lost myself in the beauty of the rugged coastal landscape. That's when the first call came from a pastor wanting to book the children for a concert.

While Louise took down the details, Suzanne let out a cheer of elation. It was happening.

By the end of the day, we had received calls from a couple more church pastors wanting to book a concert. We had also connected with my longtime friend Joan Hunter, who took it upon herself to take care of logistics. Within hours, she had located a church that had a small vacant house attached to it for use by pastors, and had secured it for the Choir children to use as a base while in the country. Then she found another fully furnished home that was used for returning missionaries and arranged for Suzanne, Louise and myself to stay there, also free of charge, during the entire tour period.

The children landed a few days later—just in time for the first concerts to begin. And by the time the ten-week concert tour was done, we had raised a hundred thousand pounds for the Somalia relief effort.

Over the years, the Choir had helped facilitate our humanitarian work around the world. Concert proceeds had provided the funding to support our work in Uganda, Kenya, Southern Sudan, Rwanda, Nigeria, Ghana and our initial efforts in South Africa.

Our Choir children had also fostered healing in other ways. During the height of the troubles in Northern Ireland between the IRA and British loyalists, we brought the African Children's Choir to Coleraine to facilitate a children's Christmas concert that included children from Killowen, the Protestant primary school I attended as a child, and St John's, a nearby Catholic school. The concert was a powerful display of peace and unity that brought Catholic and Protestant children together and eased tensions in the community.

The announcer's voice boomed over the loud speakers, bringing me back to Buckingham Palace and the historical event unfolding in front of me. It had been an incredible week leading up to this performance, with numerous television and print interviews that had generated an incredible amount of publicity for our Choir program. Now the moment we had been waiting for had finally arrived.

My eyes scanned the packed stage, taking in our Choir children that stood alongside the Military Wives Choir and dozens more musicians from other Commonwealth countries. Then my eyes rested on Lydia, who stood tall and composed, waiting for her cue.

After seconds that seemed to stretch for hours, the opening chords played and I listened along with tens of millions of other viewers as Lydia's beautiful solo voice rang out the opening words.

Lydia was one of a thousand children who had gone through our Choir program over the years—one of a thousand children who knew me as Daddy Ray, their legal guardian. And her center stage solo for the Queen of England was just one example of how far our Choir children had come. Some of our earliest Choir children—whose parents had been slaughtered in the Uganda massacre—were now serving in crucial positions throughout Africa as doctors, engineers, teachers and journalists. Others had pursued service in the ministry and several had joined our organization, working as Choir chaperones and tour leaders. I felt such an intense pride when it came to our Choir children that it was hard to put into words. They illustrated the full-circle mission we had outlined early on in the Choir program: to help African's most vulnerable children today, so they can help Africa tomorrow.

Our Choir children had demonstrated over and over again the life-transforming power of love, education and hope. But as I listened to the two-hundred strong Choir ensemble join Lydia in paying tribute to the Queen through music, it hit me that there was a lot more for our African youth to do.

I was two months away from my seventy-fifth birthday and was once again feeling the pull of my original calling: to help people around the world who were being persecuted because of their faith. The Middle East had erupted into a hotbed for extremism, and persecution against Christians was at an all-time high. They were being forced out of their homes and jobs, ridiculed, and in some cases, tortured and murdered. In Syria, both Christian and Muslim families were being caught in the crossfire of the war that was raging there. Religious persecution also continued throughout Nigeria, Sudan and other parts of Africa.

The African Children's Choir—which had been born in the wake of the horrific suffering endured by Christians in Uganda—had brought hope and healing for so many destitute African children during their time on tour. But now, as young adults, they had the power to do even more.

They were in the position to keep our work going—to keep

spreading God's love across the world and fostering hope and healing through music, education and humanitarian aid. It was just a matter of establishing a strong mentoring program that could arm our African youth with the leadership training and on-the-ground skills necessary.

The ensemble choir was nearing the end of the song, which closed the same way it opened: with Lydia's soft angelic voice delivering the final verse of the lyrics that had been written exclusively for the Queen of England.

As her voice once again took over, I thought about a conversation I'd had with British singer-songwriter Roger Whitaker early in the Choir program.

The African Children's Choir had been invited to perform with Mr. Whitaker and we had developed a friendship during our short time together. He was by far the most successful recording artist I had encountered at that time and I wanted his thoughts.

"What advice do you have for me?" I had asked him at one point. "What should I do to make sure that the Choir is a success?"

Mr. Whitaker had just smiled and shook his head.

"Ray, you don't need any advice," he had replied "It's all about passion and conviction, and you've got that. Just keep doing what you're doing and they will succeed."

Roger Whitaker's words from all those years ago vibrated through me as the song ended and the sea of flag-waving people erupted in applause and cheers.

He was right. The secret to success was passion, conviction and a fierce determination to keep moving forward, keep pushing on no matter how great the obstacles. It also required a continual resetting of the bar and an ongoing quest to achieve even more.

17

Summer 2016

THE EMAIL WAS SUCH a jolt from the past that I had to read it twice to make sure it was real.

It was from a daughter of Yanis Smits, the Baptist minister from Latvia who had fled the former Soviet Union with his family in the mid-1970s to escape persecution.

"We are holding a seventy-fifth birthday party for my dad in Toronto," Eva's note read. *"You've had such a powerful impact on our lives and we would love you to attend."*

It was early summer 2016, forty years since I had flown Yanis Smits to Washington D.C. to testify before Congress about the persecution and suffering he and other Christian leaders had been subjected to by Soviet officials. The last time I'd had contact with him was at the Vienna airport a decade later, when the Siberian Seven were finally allowed to leave the Soviet Union after years of being trapped in the US embassy in Russia.

Excitement surged through me as I dialed the associated telephone number and confirmed my attendance. After all these years, I was going to be reunited with an old friend.

During the week of the Congressional hearings, Yanis and I had grown close and he had told me about the continued struggles he faced. He said that he had managed to move to West Germany after obtaining refugee visas for his family—which included his mother, his wife, Ruth, and their twelve children. But the visas were only good for a year and the clock was ticking.

"I don't know where we're going to go," he confided over coffee one morning. "God will have to show us. There are so many in the family that it makes getting permanent visas very difficult."

I felt the familiar pull inside me as I listened to Yanis talk. I'd never helped a family get visas before and wasn't sure what was involved. But I was determined to do everything I could to help.

I invited him to come to Seattle before he returned to Europe so I could show him around the Pacific Northwest and take him to my home in Vancouver.

"Who knows?" I said. "Maybe I can help you and your family get visas into Canada."

As soon as I mentioned the idea, Yanis' face lit up. "That would be great," he replied.

There was a long pause before he continued.

"Look, I need to ask you something," he said finally. "Do you know of a place in the northwest part of America called Douglas?"

Yanis explained that a year earlier, while still in the Soviet Union, he had dreamed of the map of North America. And on the northwest corner of the map was the word 'Douglas' circled in red. He told me the dream had been so vivid that he had tried to locate the name Douglas on several maps but couldn't find it.

I'd never heard of Douglas either. But that changed a week later when we crossed the US/Canadian border.

Because Yanis was in the United States on a guest visa, he was required to go into the border crossing station for a short interview with officials. When he returned to the car a few minutes later, he was so excited he was nearly shaking.

"Ray, look at this," he said, pointing to the stamp the border official had just punched into his passport. There, in fresh blue ink, was the word Douglas.

We both stared in silence at the passport stamp, which we now understood was the name of the border crossing. It was clear God was sending a direct message that He wanted Yanis and his family in Vancouver. And I knew it was up to me to make it happen.

My friend returned to his family in West Germany and I immediately went to work. I started by approaching my local church congregation for help. We decided to establish an ad hoc committee called the Refugee Committee so that those tasked with the job of securing visas sounded official. They began making phone calls to Canadian authorities, explaining the plight of the Smits family and beginning the arduous process of securing visas for fifteen people.

In the meantime, we started searching for accommodations that could hold such a large family. It took a few months, but we eventually came across a large vacant house that was owned by a Vancouver-area church.

Though hesitant, church officials eventually agreed to let us rent it and dozens of volunteers from my church community had pulled together to turn the rundown building into a home. We scrubbed and painted the entire interior. We obtained donated furniture and appliances, hung curtains in the windows, purchased bed linens and towels, and even stocked the cupboards with food.

Everything was set to go—except the airfare.

Like the year before when I was flying him to Washington D.C. for the Congressional hearings, I had promised Yanis that tickets would be waiting for him and his family at the Dusseldorf airport.

But with only a few days to go, I still hadn't managed to secure the $5,000 necessary to pay for their flights.

As usual, Friends in the West was teetering on the edge financially and our local church congregation had already given what they could to help us cover the cost of the visas and rent, furnish and fix up the house.

With nowhere else to turn, I caught an emergency standby flight to Los Angeles, figuring the church community there might be able to raise that kind of money. But my meetings had only led to more dead ends.

I could feel the panic and desperation closing in on me as I returned to LAX and waited to catch a standby flight back to Vancouver. All I could think about was the Smits family and the desperate circumstances they were up against. All fifteen of them had survived a year in a cramped, three-room flat—holding onto the promise of a better life in Vancouver soon. But if I couldn't come up with a way to purchase the airline tickets, they were going to be stuck. And their refugee visas were days away from expiring.

I added my name to the standby list and took a seat near the gate. My heart felt like it was crushing in on itself as I contemplated the phone call I would have to make to Yanis. There had been so much joy and gratitude in his voice when I had called to tell him everything was ready to go. How could I break the news to him?

I whispered a pleading prayer for help as I waited at the gate, and continued to silently pray as the gate attendant announced that the plane was boarding. I held back for a few minutes, unable to will myself to get on the plane.

Then, just as the gate attendant was announcing the final boarding call, I heard my name over the airport loudspeaker.

"Ray Barnett, please go to a courtesy phone. Ray Barnett, there is a call waiting for you."

I rushed to a nearby bank of phones and picked up the white courtesy receiver.

"Ray, I'm so glad I caught you," Dan Wooding's voice burst through the phone line. "Can you meet me in Hollywood? I've arranged a meeting with Dean Jones."

Dan, my journalist friend from London, was in Los Angeles on business and had been trying to help me secure the funding for the plane tickets. A year earlier while on vacation in Hollywood with his family, he had run into a mutual friend who was connected to the film industry. The man had invited Dan and his family to the Warner Bros movie set to meet Dean Jones.

During the course of their conversation, the Disney star told Dan that he was a believer and had started an organization called Christian Rescue Fund that helped persecuted Christians and Jews.

After I'd returned to the airport, Dan had managed to reach Dean, and the film star had agreed to meet with us.

An hour later, Dan and I were seated across a table from the movie star in a Hollywood restaurant. He listened intently as I told him about Yanis Smits and about how his family had managed to escape relentless Soviet persecution by fleeing to West Germany. Then I told him about my mission to bring the family to Canada, about the efforts we had undergone to secure visas and a house for the family of fifteen, and about the airline tickets that I had no money to pay for.

When I was finished talking, Dean Jones pulled out his checkbook and pen.

"I want to help you bring your friends to Canada," he said. "How much do you need?"

The image of the Smits family arriving at the Vancouver house all those years ago was etched in my mind as I stepped off the plane in Buffalo, New York.

It had been such a joyful, emotional moment that we had all cried when the family first took in their new home, and I could feel those same emotions wash over me when I spotted Yanis and Ruth in the baggage claim area.

Forty years had passed since the Smits family had landed in Vancouver, and it had been thirty years since I'd run into Yanis at the Vienna airport as we both waited to greet the Siberian Seven. Yet it felt like I had seen him yesterday.

My entire body tingled with joy as we greeted each other and embraced.

"Yanis, I would have recognized you anywhere," I said, feeling the smile break open across my face. "You look just the same."

I spent the weekend with Yanis and Ruth, catching up on three decades of absence. Yanis told me he had eventually moved his family to the Toronto area to accept a position as a pastor. And after the fall of the Soviet Union, he said he had returned to Latvia, where he headed up the Baptist Union for numerous years before returning to Toronto to retire and be near his children.

When it was my turn to talk, I told them about the development of the African Children's Choir—which his son had recently hosted in a Toronto-area church—and my efforts to establish a comprehensive leadership program that could train our youth to carry on our global humanitarian relief work and keep the original Friends in the West mission moving forward.

I had left the Diamond Jubilee concert determined to put my

plan into action. My first step was to reach out to Colonel Frank Diorio with the US Marine Corps, who was married to Charlotte, an African daughter from our first Choir.

"Frank, I need to find a retired marine who can help me," I had told him. "We need a leadership training program for our young people."

Nearly two years later, Frank and I were in the mountains of Pennsylvania meeting with retired General T.S. Jones, who had developed a youth leadership academy that combined mentoring with outdoor adventure and bonding.

That meeting had led to a trip to Africa so General Jones could tour our schools, meet some of our Choir children and gain a better understanding of our program. Since that time, he had organized a team that included several wounded warriors to host Outdoor Odyssey leadership training camps at several of our schools in Africa. He had also hosted a few of our older Choir children in his base camp in Pennsylvania.

"It's still developing," I explained as I wrapped up my story. "But eventually I want to see it become a comprehensive, year-long leadership training program that really prepares our young people to carry on humanitarian relief work and continue to foster healing and hope throughout the world."

The weekend flew by. I attended Sunday morning services at the Russian church the Smits belonged to and was invited to take the podium to talk about the work I had spearheaded all those years before that had led to the release of Russian Baptist Pastor Georgi Vins.

At Yanis' birthday celebration later that evening, his children—now middle-aged adults with grown children of their own—presented me with a watch as a thank you for all I had done for their family, as well as an early eightieth birthday gift.

I was touched by the gesture. But the biggest gift came toward the end of the evening, as I was telling Yanis' daughter, Deborah, and her husband about the youth leadership program I was trying to develop, and about my growing concern over the Syrian refugees and Christians being persecuted throughout Sudan, Nigeria and the Middle East.

I'd been struggling with how to help the persecuted Christians for the past year. I was now weeks away from my eightieth birthday and some in the organization felt that I was too old to be traveling into war zones and heading up work on the ground.

But I didn't feel old. And I didn't want to stop. My ministry was what I had been put on this earth to do. When I died, I wanted to be in the field helping people, not sitting at home.

"The Church is under attack more than ever now," I told Deborah, feeling the heat surge through me as I spoke. "I don't know what the answer is. But the suffering being endured by the Syrian refugees and Christians living throughout Iraq, Sudan, Nigeria and other parts of Africa and the Middle East is horrific and I've got to do something to help."

Deborah's face twisted with emotion as she took in my words. She had been a young girl when her family fled Latvia and eventually immigrated to Canada. But I knew she understood the pain. I could see it in her eyes and hear it in her voice when she spoke.

"Ray, we want to help you," she said. "Let us know what we can do."

I was at home twelve days later when my world crashed in on me.

"Ray! Call 911!" the home health aide shouted from the next

room. "Hurry!"

I rushed to the living room and found Ruth slumped back in her easy chair. The home care worker who stopped by each morning to help Ruth shower, dress and take her medication was now hovering over her, frantically trying to revive her.

I grabbed the emergency alert necklace that hung around Ruth's neck and pushed the red button.

"It's a heart attack!" I shouted into the pager as soon as I heard a voice. "We need emergency assistance as soon as possible."

I knelt beside my wife and cradled her in my arms. I could hear the ambulance and fire truck sirens in the background speeding toward us. I wanted them to get here and bring Ruth back to me. But my gut was telling me she wouldn't make it.

The paramedics arrived and ordered me out of the room so they could work on her. I wanted to scream at them to leave me alone and let me be with my wife. Instead, I gave Ruth a final squeeze and then stumbled into the next room—half paralyzed and numb as I listened to the chaos unfolding on the other side of the wall.

I had been subconsciously preparing for this day for two years now, ever since Ruth had suffered her first heart attack, followed by another massive heart attack while at the hospital. The doctors hadn't expected her to survive and I had insisted on bringing her home.

"I don't want my wife dying in the hospital," I had told my doctor, who was on call at the hospital at the time. "She needs to be at home with her family."

We had managed to get Ruth discharged and had set up a special chair for her in the living room where she could spend her days. My children and I had taken turns caring for her ever since, with Rob serving as her primary caregiver.

We had originally thought we would have only a few more days or weeks with Ruth. But she had held on for the past two years.

Rob and Rhonda had received the emergency message and arrived at the house shortly after the paramedics landed. Rheanne was in Washington D.C. for work and was frantically searching for a flight home.

Rob, Rhonda and I held a silent vigil for Ruth as the emergency medical crew continued to work on her. Then the commotion in the next room stopped and a paramedic appeared in the doorway.

"I'm sorry," he said. "We did everything we could, but we weren't able to bring her back."

The next few days were a blur of phone calls and funeral arrangements. I was in an alternate universe. Sometimes I felt like I was floating outside my body, watching myself go through the actions. Phone calls flooded in from well-wishers, and my Facebook stream clogged with messages from people across the world, all of whom were sending their love while mourning the loss of Ruth.

Eight days after I held her in my arms for the last time, Rob, Rheanne, Rhonda and I headed to our church for a celebration of Ruth's life. I was still in so much shock I was having a hard time grasping the reality: that after fifty-five years of marriage, my wife was gone.

The crowd who gathered to pay tribute to Ruth was filled with loved ones we had known for years. Along with friends from our local church congregation, there were friends who dated back to Ruth's childhood. There were also numerous people who had either volunteered or worked for the organization over the years. And there were at least twenty members from our African Children's Choir family. Some of them had flown in from other parts of the United States, where they now lived. Omega, who had been only five years old when she joined our first Choir, traveled all the way from South Africa.

People took turns sharing stories about Ruth and the impact she'd made on their lives. The story of her quiet generosity and huge heart was repeated over and over again. While I had been on the front lines, Ruth had worked behind the scenes helping to the keep the ministry afloat. She was always knitting hats and scarves for our Choir children. And even when we were struggling to put food on our own table, she was always the first person to reach for her wallet when someone needed help.

"Where's my purse?" she would always say. "I'm sure we have something we can give."

After the tributes from people gathered in the chapel ended, the video tributes from those who couldn't be there in person started. There were numerous video messages from friends and loved ones in Africa—including one from Jemimah, an African daughter from our first Choir.

"Don't worry Mamma Ruth," she said firmly. "We will take care of Daddy Ray."

I could feel the tears welling in my eyes as her words sunk in. I don't know why, but it triggered thoughts of another funeral I had attended sixteen years earlier—the funeral of my biological mother, Margaret Barnett.

Though money was tight, I had scraped together the funds to purchase airline tickets for the entire family so we could all pay our respects to the woman who had given me birth.

Her funeral represented closure for me. I also viewed it as a way to finally meet other family members and fill in a few more puzzle pieces of my life.

But when I arrived, I discovered that the secrecy still persisted.

"I don't think you should mention that Margaret was your mother," her sister whispered to me when she saw me. "The people in our church don't know about you."

I had ignored her request and mentioned that Margaret was my mother when I had taken the microphone to speak. But I hadn't felt like her son. I felt like a stranger that had crashed a funeral. I felt empty and rejected, even with her gone.

The sound of our former Choir children making their way to the podium brought me back to the chapel. The group of them—now in their twenties and thirties—gathered in a half circle and began singing the gospel song *Soon and Very Soon*.

Their healing, comforting words wrapped around me like a cocoon. The famous lyrics by legendary Gospel Singer Song-writer Andrae Crouch talked about how we should stop crying because we would soon be seeing the King.

I listened to their beautiful voices ring out through the chapel, pride swelling inside me as I took in the poised young adults who had grown up in our Choir family.

And that's when the realization hit me: I didn't need Margaret Barnett and Bob Letson to be my family. I had my family—one I had created over the course of my life.

I had created a family with Ruth, our children Rob, Rheanne and Rhonda, and our grandchildren. I had created a family with Suzanne, Louise, Gary and the countless volunteers and supporters over the years that had made our work possible. And I had created it with the thousand-plus African children that I had become legal guardian to over the years.

These people were my family in every sense of the word. We had struggled together, fought together, laughed together and changed lives together. Now we were mourning the loss of Ruth together.

I continued to revel in my new-found realization after the funeral services, when a group of us gathered at my home so we could continue to celebrate Ruth's life and provide each other comfort.

There were nearly thirty of us and we needed food for dinner. But when I suggested that we order take-out Chinese, Margaret—my daughter from the second Choir who had flown in from Dallas—put her foot down.

"We are not getting Chinese food," she said sternly. "That's not healthy, Daddy Ray. I'm going to cook for everyone."

She and I headed to the store for groceries and soon the kitchen was filled with the aroma of prime rib and roasted vegetables.

As I watched Margaret cook, enjoyed the comforting presence of my children and grandchildren, and listened to the chatter and love around me, I thought about the word "family" and what it meant. What I now understood for certain was that it was about so much more than blood. It was about being there for each other through the ups and downs. It was about unwavering love and support. It was about the people who could make anywhere feel like home when you were with them.

My thoughts drifted to a Choir concert in Vancouver a couple years earlier.

Jemimah, who was serving as tour leader for the Choir, had closed the concert with the Celine Dion song, *Because You Loved Me*.

The song had become a source of comfort to me in recent years. During my darkest moments, it reminded me that God loved me and was always with me. More than once, those lyrics had given me the strength to pick myself up and keep going.

After the concert, Jemimah found me in the audience.

"Did you like the song, Daddy Ray?" she asked.

"Of course I did," I replied with a smile. "It's about God and his love for us."

Jemima returned my smile but slowly shook her head.

"No, Daddy Ray," she said softly. "We were singing that song about you."

EPILOGUE

November 2016

RAIN AND WIND RIPPED through the freezing air as I made my way to the Baptist Church of Coleraine—the church closest to my hotel.

The misery of the late November day matched the misery inside of me as I grappled with Ruth's death. Ten weeks had passed since I had last held my wife in my arms, and though I felt the love of my family and friends, her absence had left such a gaping hole that I couldn't stand being in Vancouver.

I had come to my homeland in hopes that I could find myself and begin to heal. And healing was on my mind as I made the decision to pull myself together and attend church service that Sunday morning.

I had never attended this church before and felt a little out of place as I took a seat near the front of the chapel. I decided to move to get out of the way and then moved again—this time to the far right corner near the back.

I settled myself onto the hard wooden pew and was preparing for the service to start when I felt a hand on my shoulder.

Startled, I turned to see who it was and found myself looking at one of my oldest childhood friends.

"Raymond, it's Margaret," she said softly.

I could feel her love and warmth radiating through me as I took in the woman I had first met as a teenager and had been lucky enough to count as a close friend ever since. I hadn't seen her in several years; but it felt like yesterday.

"We are getting old, Raymond," Margaret said, offering me a smile.

Just then, I heard someone else calling my name. It was Liz, another close friend, who happened to be walking by my row.

As with Margaret, I could feel Liz's love as she greeted me. It was as though the two of them were angels, showing up to be with me in my time of need.

The three of us met for tea after the service ended and spent the next hour sharing stories and making up for lost time. There was a shift inside of me as I immersed myself in the company and comfort of dear friends. And by the time I returned to my hotel room, I could feel the hole beginning to close.

Along with reinforcing for me that family extended well beyond blood ties, reminiscing with Margaret and Liz had started me thinking about my life journey and the most important lessons I had learned. Now, as I sat in my hotel room, I found myself reflecting deeper on the path my life had taken and on the message I wanted to share with others. I knew it came down to two simple truths: that faith required action, and that the way to make a huge impact in the world was to take it one step, and one person at a time.

As I reviewed my life, thinking about my proudest moments and accomplishments, my thoughts traveled back to the summer of 1957.

After a year at Bible college, I had decided to take some time off to work and had been filling in as a substitute pastor at churches throughout the *Saskatchewan* region. That's what I was doing in Leader, a town in southwestern *Saskatchewan*, just weeks before my twenty-first birthday.

Though I was young, I was determined to make an impact in the community, and when I heard about a family that hadn't attended church in a while, I decided to stop by their home for fellowship.

The woman who answered my knock looked to be in her late twenties or early thirties, and had so much pain in her eyes that I knew I had to get to the bottom of it.

"Is there any chance of getting a cup of coffee?" I asked after introducing myself as the new, interim pastor.

"Oh yes, please come in, Pastor Barnett," the woman said, forcing a smile as she showed me to a seat in her living room.

Within a few minutes we were in comfortable conversation, and it didn't take long to get to the heart of her pain. The woman, whose husband was away at work as a farmer, told me she had two children—a young girl and a one-year-old baby boy who wasn't responding to normal stimuli.

"I don't know what's wrong with him and I don't know what to do," she said, tears welling in her eyes.

I followed her to a basement bedroom where her baby was sleeping. She picked him up and I could tell just by looking at him that something was off. I felt the instinctual pull in my gut that has come to guide me over the years and knew I had to do everything in my power to help.

"I know what to do," I assured the woman. "I'll call the university hospital in *Saskatoon* and make an appointment. And I'll accompany you and your husband and baby so we can get some answers."

Two days later, I drove with the family to the university hospital—a three-hour journey from Leader. I got them to the medical facility, made sure they were checked in for their appointment, and then booked myself into a nearby motel to wait.

When I reunited with the couple the next day, I could feel their relief and gratitude.

"Thank you for everything," the woman said, her eyes once again moistening with tears. "The doctors were wonderful and are going to help us get the assistance we need."

I was at a conference in Moose Jaw nearly two decades later when a young woman in her mid-twenties pushed her way toward me.

"Brother Barnett, you don't know me, but my family will never forget you for helping my little brother," she said. "You made all the difference for us. We now live here in Moose Jaw because it has one of the best facilities in the world for people with mental disabilities. My brother lives there and my mother works there and gets to see him every day.

"I'm getting married in a couple of weeks," she added. "I wish you could be there to preside over it."

I think of that story when people express a sense of helplessness over the enormity of the problems facing our world. With so much suffering and need, it's easy to feel paralyzed and choose to be overwhelmed rather than to act.

But what I have learned over and over again is that every one of us—regardless of the personal challenges and adversity in our life—has the ability to transform lives and make a huge impact in this world if we act when we encounter people in need, and if we have faith that if we do everything in our power to help, God will take care of the rest.

In the months since that Sunday church service in Northern Ireland, I've continued to reflect on the lessons I've learned over the years, and about what it means to be a Christian—especially in light of the hatred and divisiveness currently gripping our world.

My heart aches when I watch the hateful words and actions unfold on the nightly news and over social media outlets. There is so much division and judgment coming from all sides, without any effort to listen and find common ground.

As I look back on my ministry, I realize the primary focus has always been the same: to foster hope and healing for those in need— regardless of faith, skin color, lifestyle choices or political views.

God doesn't want us to judge; He wants us to love. And unconditional love and compassion are critical right now.

Our world needs healing. And it's up to each of us to make it happen—one step, one shovelful, one person at a time.

-Ray Barnett, April 2017

The work continues.

Learn how you can help at www.raybarnett.com.

The Final Piece of the Puzzle

W RITING THIS BOOK MADE me realize that I was still missing a vital piece to the puzzle of my life: my sister, Mary—the daughter of my biological father, Bob Letson.

I'd looked for Mary on and off over the years without success. But when I completed the epilogue for this book in April, I could feel the ache in my heart and knew I needed to try again.

As she has done so many times over the years, Suzanne Nelson stepped in to help. She began doing research on Ancestry.com, and soon came across my father's family tree. That led to the name, Mary Letson, and Mary's married name, Swart. Suzanne tracked her to an address in Ipswich, England, and immediately called me to share the news.

I could feel the excitement surging through me as I dictated a letter to Mary, which Suzanne then emailed to a friend in Northern Ireland. We asked him to mail it from there to expedite the mailing process. I had included my phone number and email address, and waited anxiously for her response. But I heard nothing. Two weeks later the letter was returned.

I didn't know if this meant that she had moved or was no longer alive. But now that I had come this far, I couldn't turn back. The African Children's Choir was on tour in Northern England in July, and I traveled to the country to attend some of the concerts. While there, I decided to make a quick side trip to Ipswich to see what I could find out about my sister's whereabouts.

I pulled up to the modest bungalow that matched the address Suzanne had found for her and knocked on the door, hoping that the residents could tell me where she was living. But when I told the woman who answered my knock that I was trying to locate a Mary Swart who had once lived at the house, she shot me a confused look.

"Mary's my mother and this is her house," she replied.

Her announcement was so unexpected that for a minute, I couldn't speak. When I did find my words and explained who I was, it was her turn to be surprised. We both stood there—taking each other in. Then she regained her composure.

"Mum, your brother is at the door," she called into the next room.

Moments later I was ushered into the living room, where I found my sister laying in a bed that had been set up for her. Her daughter, who introduced herself as Pater, told me that Mary suffered from Parkinson's Disease and was extremely ill.

I positioned a chair next to her bed and took a seat beside her.

"Hi, Mary," I said quietly, looking at her intently. "It's your brother, Raymond. It's taken me a lifetime, but I've finally found you."

It's impossible to describe the range of emotions that swirled inside of me as I sat at my sister's bedside, exchanging stories about our childhood and life. I was so grateful that I had found her in time and that we had the opportunity to connect. But my heart felt like it was going to explode when I thought about the lifetime of memories and relationships that we had both missed out on because we hadn't found each other sooner. My little sister—the girl I'd seen only once from afar as a teenage boy—was now seventy-five years old and slowly dying, and I couldn't do anything to help her.

Before saying my goodbyes, Pater told me that she had called her brother, John, to tell him about me. "He lives an hour away but would really love to meet you," she explained. "He can come tomorrow. Can you stay an extra day?"

I booked a room at a nearby hotel and met up with my nephew and three of his children the following morning. The room buzzed with excitement and joy as we talked. Then, midway through our conversation, John made a revelation that answered one of the biggest mysteries of my life. "I am severely dyslexic and have struggled with ADHD all of my life," he said. "It runs in our family. My grandfather, Bob Letson, had the same struggles, and two of my children are dyslexic and have ADHD."

I was so floored I could hardly speak. Severe dyslexia and ADHD ran in my father's family?

Since that trip to Ipswich in July, John and I have communicated regularly via Facebook and phone conversations. He keeps me updated on Mary's condition, and recently informed me that she has been moved into a nursing home so she can access the around-the-clock care she needs.

My heart aches when I think about her health and my inability to fix it. But I'm so thankful to have found her and John, and I know they feel the same.

"I had no idea that my mother had a brother and it's been such a huge surprise," he said recently when asked about the reunion in an interview for this book. "Mum was so pleased and happy—meeting

Ray has meant the world to her. It's sad that it took so long for them to meet, but they've found each other, and that's the good thing.

"I was so happy to find out about Ray and meet him that words really can't describe it," he added. "I can't wait to get to know him a lot more."

Above: The Letson family of Killowen. Ray's biological father, Bob, is the baby sitting on his father's lap.

Below: Yanis and Ruth Smits and their family.

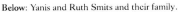

Left: Ray's biological mother, Margaret Barnett.
Below: Ray with his sister Kate (Catherine).

Above: Ray with his biological mother, Margaret Barnett, his wife, Ruth, and his sister, Kate.
Below: Members of the African Children's Choir meeting Queen Elizabeth II.

Above: Members of the African Children's Choir perform at the Queen's Jubilee Celebration in 2012.
Left: A young Ruth Barnett.

Above: Ray and Ruth in June 2016, three months before her passing. **Below:** Ray's family, pictured in June 2016.

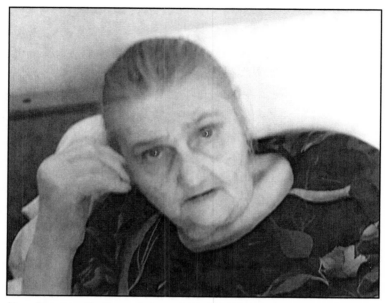

Above: Ray's sister, May Swart, who he met in July 2017. **Below:** Ray's nephew, John Swart, and his family.

ACKNOWLEDGMENTS

O VER THE COURSE OF my life I have been helped and supported by so many people that there is no way to begin to list them all.

But I want to express my sincere thanks and gratitude to all of you who have helped to support our ministry – whether through prayer, financial donations or time. Hundreds of thousands of suffering people throughout the world have benefited from your love, generosity and support.

I also want to thank all those individuals whose love, friendship and unwavering belief in me has kept me going through my darkest moments.

I especially want to thank my wife, Ruth, and my children Rob, Rheanne, and Rhonda, for their love and the immense sacrifices they have made throughout their lives so our work could continue. Ruth, who passed away on September 2nd, 2016, devoted our fifty-five years of marriage to the ministry. She wrote letters to donors, stuffed, licked and stamped tens of thousands of envelopes, knitted hats for our Choir children, oversaw fundraising drives, and opened up her heart and purse to anyone in need—all while figuring out how to stretch our meager household budget, care for our three children, and hold everything together at home.

I also want to thank Suzanne Nelson, who has devoted her life and talents to our ministry. For years she was my only staff, and worked without a salary in order to keep Friends in the West afloat. I'm not sure how I would have kept going without her.

Finally, I want to thank my extended family – the family who raised me, the biological family I have discovered, and the family of friends, colleagues and young Africans who taught me what the word "family" really means.

CPSIA information can be obtained
at www.ICGtesting.com
Printed in the USA
LVOW12*1912031217
558318LV00003B/8/P